Instructions for using

LET AUGMENTED REALITY CHANGE HOW YOU READ A BOOK

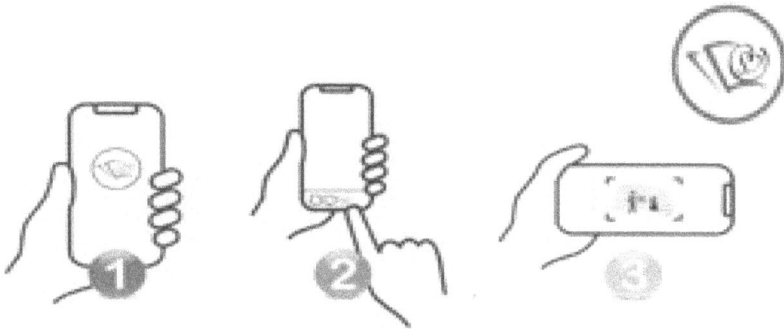

With your smartphone, iPad or tablet you can use the **Hasmark AR** app to invoke the augmented reality experience to literally read outside the book.

1. Download the **Hasmark app** from the **Apple App Store** or **Google Play**

2. Open and select the (vue) option

3. Point your lens at the full image with the and enjoy the augmented reality experience.

Go ahead and try it right now with this image:

FEEL GREAT IN 28!

ENDORSEMENTS

Barbara Diaz de Leon's 'Feel Great in 28!' is a triumph of holistic health and wellness, expertly tailored for those navigating the intricacies of midlife and beyond, especially while managing chronic conditions. Diaz de Leon's 28-Day Kickstart Plan is not just a program—it's a compassionate guide back to oneself, promising a rejuvenation of spirit and a liberation from the weight that life sometimes places upon us. With her insightful wisdom, Diaz de Leon doesn't just offer a temporary solution; she provides a sustainable approach to living with vitality and joy. This book is an essential read for anyone looking to reclaim their health and zest for life. It's a beacon of hope and a testament to the strength that resides within us all to make positive, lasting changes.

- Peggy McColl,
New York Times Best-Selling Author
http://peggymccoll.com

"Feel Great 28'" is an invaluable resource for women navigating the challenging and transformative phase of menopause. Authored by Barbara Diaz de Leon, this book offers a comprehensive guide to understanding the impact of menopause on overall well-being. It provides practical strategies for maintaining a healthy lifestyle during this crucial period, focusing on regular exercise and a positive psychological mindset to drive you to success.

One of the book's greatest strengths is its emphasis on education and empowerment. Barbara takes a holistic approach, not only addressing the physical changes that occur during menopause but also delving into the emotional and psychological aspects.

The nutritional guidance presented in this book is evidence-based and highly informative. It covers a wide range of topics, including the importance of a balanced diet, with delicious, nutrient-packed meals that are satisfying and delicious, helping to stabilize blood sugar and reduce cravings. What sets this book apart from others is its compassionate and empathetic tone. Barbara understands women's challenges and struggles during menopause, and the book is infused with understanding and support.

- Dr. Daniela Steyn,
Bestselling author of "Thrive Through Menopause"

"Feel Great in 28!" is a health-boosting plan created by certified health coach Barbara Diaz de Leon. Filled with ideas you can use, her book is based on everything she learned about her own body and its needs as she struggled over some 15 years to overcome (successfully!) a host of symptoms. This plan is designed to help you reset your body's physical state so you can move forward in the best possible health and soar through menopause feeling even better in your later years than you did in your 40s!

- Judy O'Beirn
President Hasmark Publishing International

FEEL GREAT IN 28!

A 28-DAY KICKSTART PLAN
to release unwanted weight and get your
zest back — even during midlife beyond
with chronic disease along for the ride!

By

Barbara Diaz de Leon, RN

Hasmark
PUBLISHING
INTERNATIONAL

Published by
Hasmark Publishing International
www.hasmarkpublishing.com

Disclaimer

This book is designed to provide information and motivation to our readers. It is sold with the understanding that the publisher is not engaged to render any type of medical, psychological, legal, or any other kind of professional advice. The content of each article is the sole expression and opinion of its author, and not necessarily that of the publisher. No warranties or guarantees are expressed or implied by the publisher's choice to include any of the content in this volume. Neither the publisher nor the individual author shall be liable for any physical, psychological, emotional, financial, or commercial damages, including, but not limited to, special, incidental, consequential or other damages. Our views and rights are the same: You are responsible for your own choices, actions, and results. This book is for educational and informational purposes only. The content of this book should not be interpreted as medical or professional advice. The reader should carefully evaluate the information provided and consult with a licensed health-care professional before making any decisions or taking any actions based on the content of this book. All the information has been checked to the best of our ability to be factually correct at the time of print. New research gets published often. The North American Menopause Society's website is a good source to find the latest research on menopause. This book does not replace a visit with your health-care provider. Do not ignore advice from your health-care provider because of something you have read in this book.

Permission should be addressed in writing to Barbara Diaz de Leon at coach@dailywellnessforyou.com

Editor: Murray Lewis (murray@hasmarkpublishing.com)
Cover Design: Anne Karklins (anne@hasmarkpublishing.com)
Interior Layout: Amit Dey (amit@hasmarkpublishing.com)

ISBN: 978-1-77482-249-4
ISBN 10: 1774822490

Hasmark
INTERNATIONAL

DEDICATION

To all of the amazing Functional Medicine and Integrative Medicine practitioners who are helping women to heal and live their best lives.

ACKNOWLEDGMENTS

*T*o my incredible support system, my loving family and dear friends, you are my world! Your unwavering encouragement and belief in me have been the fuel that kept me going.

Debra Muth, ND, NP: Your expertise and dedication in functional medicine have been more than just professional support; they have been a true partnership in my health journey. Your refusal to settle for surface-level answers and your deep commitment to understanding the underlying causes have been pivotal in navigating the complexities of my health. Your collaborative approach has not only guided me towards healing but also empowered me with knowledge and insight. I am immensely grateful for your unwavering support and invaluable partnership.

Justin Marchegiani, DC: Your approach to functional medicine has been a beacon in my health journey. Going beyond initial 'normal' test results, you have been a pillar of accountability, keeping me committed to the path of healing and wellness. This aspect of your care has proven invaluable, not only improving my health but also fostering a sense of responsibility and empowerment in my journey. Thank you for being not just a doctor, but a true partner and guide in this journey.

Nadia Matter, my writing "accomplishment" partner: your boundless encouragement and inspiration went above and beyond. You filled my heart with love and motivation.

Penelope Yiatrou, my business accountability partner: thank you for keeping me on track with my business activities during the writing process. Your support was invaluable.

Elle Russ: you played a pivotal role in transforming me into a confident force. Your influence on my life goes beyond words. Thank you!

Peggy McColl: your outstanding guidance has been nothing short of amazing. Your generous spirit and giving nature have had a profound impact on me, and I am forever grateful.

Marejo Ramsey and Lisa Burns: not only are you my cherished gym companions, but you're also dear friends whose support extends far beyond our fitness adventures. My affection for and gratitude to both of you run deep. Much love to you both!

TABLE OF CONTENTS

FOREWORD

*T*o the Courageous Health Seeker,

As you embark on the transformative journey laid out in these pages, I extend a heartfelt welcome and a virtual embrace of encouragement. You are not alone in this quest for vitality and well-being. The story within these pages is not just a narrative; it's a reflection of a shared experience that resonates deeply with many, including myself.

This book is a labor of love and a testament to Barbara's resilience, speaking directly to those who find themselves navigating the often-tumultuous waters of midlife health challenges. Through personal struggles and triumphs, Barbara crafts a narrative that transcends the typical health guide. It's a story of overcoming, rediscovering oneself amid the complexities of bodily changes, and finding solace and strength in taking control of one's health.

Having endured over fifteen years of health issues that ranged from chronic fatigue to high blood pressure and beyond, the author's journey mirrors the experiences of many. The frustrations with conventional medical responses, the sense of being misunderstood, and the relentless pursuit of answers are themes that will resonate with every reader who has ever felt dismissed or misunderstood by the healthcare system.

But this book is more than a recounting of challenges. It is a beacon of hope, a guide that illuminates the path to reclaiming health and vitality through sustainable and personalized strategies. It is a testament to the power of resilience and the transformative potential of informed intentional health choices.

As a colleague and a witness to Barbara's journey, I can attest to the profound impact that this approach to health can have. I have had the pleasure of watching her transformation in her own life and the lives of many others. This book is not just a compilation of advice; it is a companion on your journey, offering wisdom, empathy, and practical strategies that cater to the uniqueness of each individual's journey.

You are about to embark on a path that may challenge you, inspire you, and ultimately lead you to a place of greater health and understanding. Embrace this journey with an open heart and a willing spirit, and let this book be your guide to a healthier, more vibrant you.

In health and solidarity,
Deb Muth, ND, NP

PREFACE

*H*ey there, Beautiful Health Seeker!

First things first—let me give you a big virtual hug and a round of applause for taking the leap to optimizing your health. You're on a fantastic journey, and I'm thrilled to be a part of it with you.

Now, let me tell you a bit about this book and why it's so close to my heart.

I wrote these pages with the intention of giving *real* hope to all the inspiring women out there in midlife and beyond who might be struggling with some pesky health challenges. You know, those moments when you feel drained of energy, your joints are acting up, your digestion is out of whack, and those stubborn pounds just won't budge. Not to mention the brain fog, the sleep issues, and all those mysterious symptoms that came knocking when midlife decided to show up.

I get it, I really do. I suffered through over fifteen years of dealing with chronic fatigue, high blood pressure, digestion troubles, brain fog, joint pain, mood swings, and unwanted weight gain. And let me tell you, feeling down and losing my zest for life was the cherry on top of that not-so-delicious cake.

But guess what? When I sought help from doctors, their answers were pretty underwhelming. "You're fine," they said. "Just getting older," they said. And my favorite, "You need to eat less and exercise more." Oh, come on. Really?

Some even suggested it was all in my mind, and that's when the antidepressants came into play. Not my idea of a solution!

Don't get me wrong—I believe in the power of the mind, and I'm all for therapy. But deep down, I knew there was a physical issue at the core of it all. My mental state was a result of my health struggles, not the cause.

If any of this sounds familiar to you, and if you're looking for sustainable solutions, then you've landed in the right place.

I'm eternally grateful that I held on to a tiny glimmer of hope, an intuitive sense that there had to be a way out of this mess. And boy, did I find it!

I tried those popular weight-loss programs, and sure, I shed some pounds. But the fatigue was still there, and so were the medications, the brain fog, and everything else. I could fit into smaller jeans, but that didn't make me any healthier.

And the worst part? When I quit those programs, the weight came right back. They weren't a sustainable solution at all.

Plus, let's face it: those programs were just plain unhealthy. While they offered a few "good" things, they also gave me the green light to chow down on loads of processed junk. No wonder they didn't work.

But enough of the negative stuff. The great news is that I found my way out of that desperate, messy situation, and I successfully transformed both my body and mind.

This life-changing experience sparked a fire within me, leading me to become a Certified Health Coach, eager to help other incredible women like you achieve optimal health in a sustainable way.

And you can do it! No matter whether you're dealing with menopause, chronic illnesses, or any other challenges—I managed to turn things around even in the middle of menopause, while juggling autoimmune issues, Lyme disease, high blood pressure, and some genetic detox concerns. And my clients have seen incredible success, too.

We're all unique, and that's why I'm a big fan of customized plans. We need to work with what makes each of us special. But don't worry; there are some commonalities that have contributed to my success and that of my clients, and I'm eager to share those with you so you can kickstart your journey to *great* health.

Oh, and just a quick heads up: throughout this book, you'll see me mention certain companies and product names. Let me assure you, I'm not affiliated with any of them, and I don't get any compensation for giving them a shout-out. I just genuinely like to recommend quality products that can help you on your path to better health.

So, are you ready to say goodbye to those ineffective diet plans and finally make a positive change in your health, once and for all?

I see that nod and that enthusiasm—you go, girl! Let's dive into this adventure together and get you on the road to feeling amazing. Let's go!

PART ONE

What on Earth
Is Happening to Me?

CHAPTER 1

❧❦❧

MY DOCTOR TELLS ME I'M FINE—UGH!

"*Y*ou're fine," my doctor said as he reviewed my lab results. But I was anything but fine. I had been dealing with constant tiredness, digestive problems, brain fog, putting on weight, and feeling achy all over. It felt as though I couldn't remember a thing.

As if that wasn't frustrating enough, my doctor hit me with the classic advice: "Just eat less and exercise more" and "Reduce your stress." Yeah, great, but how am I supposed to manage that when I can't just drop everything and escape to a serene yoga retreat? And to top it off, he told me that these things are just part of getting older. Really? I was hearing this in my mid-thirties!

Have you experienced something similar when you went to your doctor with complaints such as:

- Feeling tired or even exhausted all the time?
- Struggling with unexplained weight gain that refuses to budge?

- Watching your hair fall out?
- Dealing with body aches and pains, even without an injury?
- Battling feelings of anxiety and depression?
- Experiencing poor sleep quality, leaving you drained?
- Struggling with memory issues and brain fog?
- Suffering from digestive troubles such as bloating, constipation, or diarrhea?
- Frequently getting headaches, making life harder?

I want to make it clear that I'm not here to bash doctors or other health-care practitioners with good intentions. Let's cut them some slack.

However, I must express immense gratitude to those health-care professionals who went above and beyond by diving into functional and integrative medicine modalities. They put in the time and effort to study beyond their conventional training, and that's commendable.

Most licensed health-care practitioners enter their field with a genuine desire to help people. But the system limits them. They have to follow industry standards to ensure insurance coverage and get paid. Plus, they have only 15–30 minutes for a new patient visit and 10–20 minutes for follow-up appointments. How can they truly understand your situation and have an interactive discussion in such limited time? On top of that, they often don't delve into advanced testing as functional medicine providers do, which is why they might miss some crucial health issues in conventional lab work.

Other factors hinder their ability to provide the best care, such as inadequate nutrition knowledge and the pressure to see as many patients as possible, leading to excessive documentation for billing purposes, even if it's not necessarily relevant to the patient's care. I've seen this firsthand during my time working in medical billing and compliance.

But enough about them. What you need are solutions, and you need them now. That's why you have this book, and it's a great first step.

One thing I really want to ask of you right now is to believe in the possibility of better health and feeling amazing again. Even if it's just a tiny, flickering hope, hold on to it. That little flame has the power to grow and ignite change in your life. Trust me—I held onto a glimmer of hope that one day I'd feel like a human again, and I'm so grateful that I didn't let it fade away.

You absolutely have what it takes to turn things around. So, let's dive in and make this transformation happen. This journey is all about simple nutrition, movement, and lifestyle habits that can create a massive positive shift in your health. You've got this. Let's make it a reality together!

CHAPTER 2

✥

LET'S MAKE COMMON CHRONIC DISEASES LESS COMMON!

*L*et's talk about something that needs to be said loud and clear: the fact that certain health conditions are common doesn't make them normal.

If I had a dollar for every time I heard someone dismiss chronic diseases as just a natural part of aging, I'd be a gazillionaire by now. But that's not the truth we're going to accept.

We're diving into some of the most prevalent lifestyle diseases that have unfortunately become all too familiar. Brace yourself, because it's time to shed light on these sneaky culprits:

Cardiovascular Disease: This category covers heart disease, heart attacks, and stroke, often tied to factors such as high blood pressure, high cholesterol, smoking, lack of physical activity, and poor diet.

Type 2 Diabetes: This chronic condition occurs when the body becomes resistant to insulin or doesn't produce enough of it. It's often linked to obesity, physical inactivity, and poor diet.

Hypertension (High Blood Pressure): This silent trouble-maker can lead to severe health complications, including heart disease, stroke, and kidney disease. Poor diet, obesity, and physical inactivity play their parts here.

Liver Disease: Chronic liver issues such as non-alcoholic fatty liver disease (NAFLD) and alcoholic liver disease are closely associated with excessive alcohol consumption, obesity, and poor diet.

Kidney Disease: Conditions like chronic kidney disease can be influenced by hypertension, diabetes, obesity, and unhealthy lifestyle habits, such as smoking and poor diet. Lack of physical activity can also contribute to several risk factors for kidney disease.

Notice a common thread in all of these? Poor diet and physical inactivity seem to pop up everywhere! And let's not forget that unmanaged chronic stress and poor sleep quality can also play a significant role in these lifestyle diseases. (We'll discuss stress and sleep in more depth in later chapters.)

Now, I want to shine a spotlight on something called "metabolic syndrome." It's a group of conditions that pave the way for heart disease, diabetes, stroke, and other health issues. Metabolic syndrome becomes a concern when someone has three or more of these risk factors: high blood glucose, low levels of HDL ("good") cholesterol, high triglycerides, a large waist circumference, and high blood pressure. This syndrome is often tied to lifestyle factors such as obesity, physical inactivity, poor diet (especially a diet high in processed foods and added sugars), and insulin resistance. But fret not, because we'll delve into how to manage and improve these factors in the upcoming chapters.

A quick word about autoimmune diseases (rheumatoid arthritis, Hashimoto's thyroiditis, celiac disease, Crohn's disease, ulcerative colitis, multiple sclerosis, and more). Many folks are led to believe that nutrition and lifestyle changes won't make a difference in their symptoms. It's not true. Countless people, including me and many of my clients, have experienced incredible outcomes by transforming their nutrition and lifestyle. While this book isn't exclusively about autoimmune diseases, the approaches recommended here can be a fantastic starting point to improve your health. If you're interested, check out Dr. Terry Wahls's books; she's a physician with her own inspiring story of transformation and multiple sclerosis.

Finally, let's briefly talk about genetics. Yes, there are certain diseases with strong genetic connections, but here's where it gets exciting—have you heard of "epigenetics"?

Influenced by our environment and lifestyle choices, epigenetics is all about how our DNA can be modified without changing the sequence of our genes. Imagine chemical tags that can be added to or removed from our DNA, affecting how our genes behave. Factors such as diet, stress, exercise, and exposure to toxins can act as switches, turning genes on or off, and can have a lasting impact on our health. So, even with "bad genetics," you have the power to influence your genes and make a difference. It's truly empowering!

And for those of you who feel miserable all the time but hear the infamous "you're fine" or "it's just part of aging" from your practitioners, don't lose hope. I've been there, and many of my clients have, too.

Sometimes, practitioners don't order the necessary in-depth tests due to time constraints and insurance limitations. In addition, conditions like chronic Lyme disease can be challenging to identify in tests. But no matter the reason, there's so much you can do.

So, keep that hope alive and read on. We've got a world of solutions and empowerment ahead of us.

CHAPTER 3

⋖◈⋗

HELTER-SKELTER HORMONES!

*A*ll right, it's time for a quick and painless lesson on hormones—no worries, no pop quiz at the end!

I won't delve into the intricate details of each hormone here; that could fill a library. However, if you're eager to learn more, I've provided some fantastic recommendations in the Resource section of this book (check out "Appendix C").

For now, we'll focus on two hormones that have my special attention: thyroid hormones and progesterone. Let's take a journey back in time and start with a seemingly healthy woman in her thirties. That isn't exactly midlife, but it's an essential starting point because it was the beginning of my own hormone horror, and it resonates with many other women, too, unfortunately.

During that time, I had no idea about my underlying hormone issues. Additionally, my conventional doctor never bothered to do a complete thyroid panel or check my female hormones. Little did I know that not addressing these concerns would lead me to suffer from constant fatigue and a range of other symptoms for over fifteen years. As a result, I ended up having an early hysterectomy and couldn't bear children.

Let's start with thyroid hormones, particularly when you're hypothyroid (having an underactive thyroid).

Common symptoms of hypothyroidism include but aren't limited to:

- Fatigue (feeling this most, if not all, of the time)
- "Unexplained" weight gain
- Inability to lose weight
- Depression
- Infertility
- Low libido
- Body pain (muscle and/or joint)
- Brain fog, memory, and concentration issues
- Feeling cold often, with cold hands and feet, and low body temperature
- Constipation
- Hair loss

Unfortunately, many conventional doctors don't order a complete thyroid panel, and this is a big deal. They typically check only your thyroid-stimulating hormone (TSH) and sometimes thyroxine (T4) levels, but that isn't enough for a complete thyroid evaluation.

TSH signals your thyroid to produce thyroid hormones. And when released into the bloodstream, T4 gets converted into the active thyroid hormone triiodothyronine (T3). T3 is the superstar that regulates your body's metabolism, energy usage, and various vital functions.

Problems arise when your body has trouble converting T4 to T3. If your doctor checks only TSH and T4 and prescribes levothyroxine (commonly known as Synthroid), which is essentially T4 only, it might not resolve your symptoms if you're a "poor T4 converter."

Factors such as deficiencies of nutrients (such as selenium and iodine), hormonal imbalances, certain medications, and chronic illnesses can all play a role in this conversion process. Also, a comprehensive thyroid panel should include checking for antibodies related to Hashimoto's thyroiditis, an autoimmune condition.

Low progesterone levels can also cause issues, including estrogen dominance, which can lead to various troublesome symptoms such as bloating, fibrocystic breast lumps, heavy and painful periods, mood swings, headaches, weight gain, hair loss, fibroids, decreased sex drive, anxiety, and depression.

If you find yourself experiencing any of these symptoms, it's crucial to get your female hormones checked, preferably by a functional medicine or integrative medicine health-care practitioner. They can look into other possible hormone-related issues and provide a more holistic approach to your care.

Now, let's briefly touch on Hormone Replacement Therapy (HRT). HRT can help manage symptoms associated with hormonal changes in midlife and beyond, such as hot flashes, mood swings, and sleep disturbances. It can also help prevent bone loss— crucial during menopause to reduce the risk of osteoporosis.

For some, bioidentical hormones may be a preferable option, as they mimic more closely hormones produced naturally in the body. Ultimately, the decision about HRT should be made in consultation with your licensed health-care practitioner, who can guide you toward the most appropriate treatment for your individual needs.

However, remember that there's a lot you can do beyond HRT to balance hormones and alleviate associated symptoms. Good nutrition and lifestyle habits, such as proper sleep, stress management, and balanced exercise, can all play a significant role in hormone health. We'll explore more about these empowering solutions in the upcoming chapters. Keep reading, and you'll discover the tools you need to take charge of your health journey.

PART TWO

The Whole Health Approach: More Than Just Food and Exercise

CHAPTER 4

❦

WHAT ARE YOU FEEDING YOUR MIND?

*W*hat story are you telling yourself? Is your mindset misleading you? These are questions that hold significant importance because what you feed your mind plays a crucial role in your health and weight-loss journey. It matters, and it matters *a lot!*

In a world prone to negativity, cultivating a positive mindset and positive beliefs becomes essential. The good news is that you have control over your thoughts. All this "mind stuff" is powerful, and let's start by exploring the placebo effect to emphasize this point.

The placebo effect is a real phenomenon in which a person experiences a beneficial health outcome simply because they anticipate that an intervention will help. Numerous studies have proven the power of the placebo effect, and even pharmaceutical companies take it into account when evaluating the effectiveness of new drugs. The mind's beliefs and expectations can have a significant impact on the body's response.

On the other hand, there's the nocebo effect—a patient experiences side effects or symptoms just because they believe they may occur. Once again, this illustrates the power of the mind and thoughts in shaping our experiences.

The words we use are equally powerful. Like thoughts, words have significant influence over our mindset. Here are two simple but impactful suggestions you can put into action today:

1. Replace "I have to" with "I choose to" or "I get to." *Having* to do something can feel burdensome, but shifting to a positive perspective can change the energy and make it feel like a choice rather than an obligation.

2. Replace "I'll try" with more decisive statements like "I'm going to," "I will," "I commit to," or "I plan to." This removes the possibility of "not having to do it" and instills a more determined mindset.

Cultivating a positive mindset brings a myriad of benefits to your health journey:

- **Motivation and resilience:** A positive outlook provides motivation and enhances resilience, enabling you to overcome challenges and persistently work toward your goals.

- **Problem-solving and creativity:** A positive mindset encourages open and expansive thinking, leading to creative approaches to overcoming obstacles.

- **Improved self-belief and confidence:** Positive thinking boosts self-belief and confidence, empowering you to take decisive actions aligned with your goals.

- **Enhanced emotional well-being:** A positive mindset reduces stress and anxiety, creating mental space and energy for focus and determination.

While cultivating positivity, it's also essential to acknowledge negative emotions that may arise. Don't suppress or ignore them; instead, acknowledge their presence, seek balance, and shift toward a solution-oriented outlook. Look for lessons and blessings in challenging situations.

Practicing gratitude is another powerful tool to foster a positive mindset. Gratitude helps shift focus away from complaints and negative experiences, improving emotional well-being. You can start by writing down three things you're grateful for each day and intentionally pondering them.

One more critical aspect of mindset revolves around understanding your "why." Knowing why your health and weight loss goals matter to you is a game-changer. People who achieve and maintain their health goals are clear on their reasons for transformation. Identifying your "why" gives you daily motivation and keeps your attention on the right thing.

Remember, developing a habit of positivity takes practice, but the effort is worth it. It can significantly affect your ability to reach your goals and improve your overall well-being. These activities cost nothing and you can easily implement them today. Don't put them off; start fostering a positive mindset now to empower your health journey.

CHAPTER 5

⚜

WHERE DO YOU LAND ON THE "STRESS-O-METER"?

*S*tress is a serious matter that deeply affects your health and weight-loss journey. Don't underestimate the importance of this chapter. Effective stress management can be a game-changer when it comes to achieving your health goals. Let's explore what stress is and how it impacts your body.

Stress, as defined by WebMD, is the body's response to harmful situations, whether real or perceived. When you feel threatened, your body activates the "fight-or-flight" response, preparing you to take action and protect yourself. Your heart rate increases, breathing quickens, muscles tense, and blood pressure rises—all signs that you're ready to face the challenge.

It's essential to recognize that stressors vary from person to person. What may seem overwhelming to one might not bother another. Interestingly, as clients adopt healthier lifestyles, their stress tolerance often increases due to improved gut health (more on this later in the nutrition section).

While short bursts of stress can be beneficial, *chronic* stress is what we should watch out for. Unfortunately, we can't eliminate all stressors—such as difficult co-workers or heavy traffic— from our lives, but we can manage our response to them and learn to handle them better. Stress management, not stress reduction, is the goal here.

Before we explore stress management tools, let's understand what chronic stress can do to your body. According to the American Psychological Association, the prolonged activation of the stress response system, with increased cortisol and other stress hor-mones, disrupts nearly all bodily processes. This leaves you vul-nerable to various physical and mental health issues, including anxiety, depression, digestive problems, headaches, muscle ten-sion, heart disease, high blood pressure, stroke, sleep disturbances, weight gain, and impaired memory and concentration. Stress can be deadly!

Now that you know the consequences of unmanaged chronic stress, you understand the urgency of addressing it. The good news is that even if you can't attend a yoga retreat every weekend, there are practical ways to manage stress.

The key is to activate the "parasympathetic" state, a calming and healing state for your body. Even a few moments in this state can make a significant difference for your body and mind. Here are some stress-management techniques you can implement:

1. **Breathing practices:** One of the simplest techniques is box breathing—inhale for 4 counts, hold for 4 counts, exhale for 4 counts, and hold for 4 counts. Another option is simply take 5 to 10 deep, slow breaths.

2. **Meditation:** Just ten minutes a day of focusing on your breath, or using guided meditation apps like Insight Timer or Calm, can promote calmness, enhanced immunity, lower blood pressure, better sleep, and greater happiness.

3. **Epsom salt baths:** A five-minute soak can help your body relax. Be cautious if you have low blood pressure and always be mindful when getting out of the tub.

4. **Essential oils and CBD oil:** Vetiver, frankincense, lavender, and CBD oil can aid in stress management. Ensure you get quality oils and be careful with essential oils around pets.

5. **Yoga and stretching:** Even ten minutes of daily practice can significantly reduce stress. You can follow online videos for various levels of practice.

6. **Chamomile and green tea:** These teas have calming properties. Caffeinated green tea can provide a gentle boost and calmness.

7. **Nature:** Being in nature or even looking at the sky through a window can lower cortisol levels.

8. **Smile:** Studies suggest that smiling during stressful moments can reduce the body's stress response, even if you don't feel happy.

Remember, stress management is as crucial as the food you eat. In the 28-Day Kickstart Plan in Part Four, we'll cover stress management tools to support your journey to a healthier and happier life. Stress doesn't have to be an insurmountable obstacle; with the right techniques, you can conquer it and move closer to your health goals.

CHAPTER 6

◈

ARE YOU COUNTING SHEEP?

"*I* don't have enough time to sleep more." How often have we heard or even said this ourselves? In our busy lives, it's easy to prioritize work, responsibilities, and entertainment over sleep. But what if we've got it all wrong? What if, instead of not having enough time to sleep, we don't have enough time *not* to sleep?

Sleep deficiency is more than just feeling tired all the time. It can have serious consequences for our health and well-being. Let's take a closer look at some of the effects of chronic sleep deprivation:

1. **Chronic health problems:** Heart disease, kidney disease, high blood pressure, diabetes, stroke, obesity, and depression are linked to poor sleep patterns.

2. **Increased risk of injury:** Lack of sleep can lead to accidents and injuries due to impaired alertness and slow reaction times.

3. **Mood swings:** Sleep deficiency can cause irritability, moodiness, and emotional imbalance.

4. **Weight and muscle issues:** Both weight loss and muscle gain can be significantly affected by inadequate sleep.

5. **Lack of focus and attention:** Reduced sleep leads to difficulty concentrating and shortened attention spans.

6. **Impaired memory and decision-making:** Sleep deprivation affects cognitive functions, including memory and judgment.

7. **Reduced work efficiency and motivation:** Quality sleep is essential for peak performance and productivity.

Quality sleep is an absolute necessity for our physical and mental well-being. Most people require seven to eight hours of quality sleep to function optimally. So, it's time to shift our perspective and embrace the mantra, "I don't have time *not* to sleep." Giving ourselves permission to sleep is not laziness; it's the pathway to a healthy and fulfilling life.

To improve sleep quality, here are some helpful tips:

1. **Establish a "screen curfew":** Avoid electronic devices beginning at least an hour before bedtime. Blue screens can disrupt our natural sleep-wake cycle.

2. **Limit caffeine intake:** Avoid consuming caffeine after 2 p.m. (or earlier if you're sensitive) to ensure better sleep quality.

3. **Moderate alcohol consumption:** Alcohol may make you drowsy initially, but it disrupts the overall quality of your sleep.

4. **Read calming material before bed:** Opt for soothing fiction or relaxation techniques rather than stimulating nonfiction.

5. **Practice deep breathing:** Take 10–15 deep breaths before bedtime to relax your body and mind.

6. **Create a dark sleep environment:** Invest in blackout window blinds or use an eye mask to promote deep REM sleep.

7. **Set the right temperature:** Aim for a room temperature between 60 and 67 degrees Fahrenheit (15 to 19 degrees Celsius).

8. **Use earplugs and soothing sounds:** Block external noises and consider using sleep apps with calming sounds.

9. **Maintain a consistent sleep schedule:** Stick to the same bedtime and wake-up time every day, including weekends.

10. **Embrace natural light exposure:** Get outside during the day to regulate your body's production of melatonin.

11. **Take a relaxing bath:** A warm bath with Epsom salts can promote relaxation before bedtime.

For night-shift workers, implementing these tips becomes even more critical to ensure regular and sufficient quality sleep.

Remember, sleep is not a luxury; it's a necessity for our physical and mental well-being. By prioritizing quality sleep, you can achieve more, be happier, and become the best version of yourself. So, give yourself the gift of restful slumber and let your body revitalize for a healthier and more fulfilling life.

CHAPTER 7

⚜

"I DON'T HAVE ENOUGH TIME IN THE DAY!"

*D*o you often catch yourself saying, "I don't have enough time in the day"? Well, it's time to pause and reconsider those words. Remember how we emphasized the importance of language in "Chapter 4"? The way we phrase things matters, and this phrase can be indicative of a deeper issue: inadequate boundary-setting skills.

Setting boundaries is a crucial and often overlooked aspect of a healthy lifestyle. Boundaries apply to various aspects of our lives, including our time and energy. Let's explore how boundaries impact our well-being, both personally and in our interactions with others.

First, we have self-boundaries, which involve setting appropriate limits for ourselves. Examples can be as simple as maintaining a consistent bedtime of 10:00 p.m. every night, shutting off all screens one hour before bedtime, avoiding caffeine after 12:00 p.m., resisting the vending machine at work, or not hitting the snooze button to prevent being late for work. These small self-boundaries create a foundation for a healthier lifestyle.

Equally important are boundaries with others. Many of us lead busy lives, juggling work and family responsibilities. While occasional busy periods are understandable, recurring patterns of overworking are not healthy. If you find yourself constantly working overtime with no support from management, it's time to voice your concerns. Chronic overworking takes a toll on your emotional, mental, and eventually physical well-being. It's crucial to strike a balance between work and personal life.

Boundaries can also be essential in our personal relationships. While it's natural to want to help and support loved ones, being everything to everyone can come at a high cost to yourself. Saying "no" doesn't make you selfish; it's an act of self-care and self-preservation. You don't need to justify your "no" with a lengthy explanation. Simply setting a healthy boundary is enough.

Changing long-established patterns may be challenging, and your loved ones might not immediately embrace your newfound boundaries. Give them time to adjust. Remember, this is about creating a healthier you. As you start feeling better and enjoying the peace that comes from a balanced life, you'll find that saying "no" becomes more comfortable and empowering.

Choosing to set boundaries now might be tough, but it's about prioritizing your future well-being. Consider the saying, "Choose your hard." It may be challenging now to set boundaries, but it will lead to an easier and healthier future compared to the hardship of chronic illness due to neglecting your own needs.

Setting healthy boundaries sends a powerful message to yourself and others. It's a declaration that you value your well-being and deserve respect. By maintaining appropriate boundaries, you protect your physical, mental, and emotional health, enabling a better work-life balance.

Embracing boundaries will allow you to make time for your healthy habits, contributing to an overall healthier and happier you. Remember, you deserve to prioritize your well-being, and boundaries are the foundation for a healthier life.

PART THREE

This Is a Starvation-Free and Chronic Cardio-Free Zone!

CHAPTER 8

꠸❦꠸

DITCH THE DIET FADS AND EMBRACE NOURISHING NUTRITION

*B*eware of those popular diet programs!

Let's talk about these programs and why you should approach them with caution. You've probably come across many of these diets, and while they may provide some short-term results, they often fail in the long run. Many people find themselves gaining back the weight they lost once they stop following these programs. I've heard this story countless times from my prospects and clients, and I've experienced it myself.

The problem with these diets is that they can create an unhealthy relationship with food by emphasizing strict tracking and rigid rules. While some changes will inevitably occur when you start a new program, there's so much more to great nutrition than assigning points to every food item. These plans are often not sustainable in the long term, leading to weight regain and frustration.

The truth is, we are all unique individuals with different needs and reactions to foods. What works for one person may not work for another. For example, while dairy may be a healthy option for some, it can be highly inflammatory for others, especially those with autoimmune conditions.

Also, it's important to avoid highly inflammatory foods, especially processed foods made with high-fructose corn syrup and industrial seed or vegetable oils (such as soybean oil), even if you "have enough points left for the day" for them.

I get it; these popular diet plans can be tempting. I've tried some myself, including the ones based on points and packaged snacks. While on these plans, I was hungry *all the time*.

And yes, I did lose weight—temporarily. But I still had all of my other health issues, including my chronic fatigue, high blood pressure (I still required two prescription medications for it), body-wide joint pain, brain fog, digestive issues, sleep issues, and mood imbalances (in other words, I was not very pleasant). I was able to wear smaller jeans—hooray—but as I said, the weight loss was temporary because these plans are not sustainable. The lost weight came back.

I hear stories like mine over and over again.

However, when I avoided foods that were inflammatory and added to my diet nutrient-dense, blood-sugar balancing, anti-inflammatory, and gut-healing foods, my body responded beautifully. I lost weight and kept it off—without starving, without tracking! Not one point tracked, not one calorie counted!

That said, calories do indeed matter. But for us ladies in perimenopause, menopause, or post-menopause, or those with autoimmune conditions at any age, getting inflammation down is one of the keys to great health. Flooding your body with nutrient-dense foods and avoiding inflammatory foods is both effective and delicious. Interestingly, with my clients, many don't track food at all, except protein (more on that later), and they feel liberated by this. Most of them had tried all these points and tracking programs without lasting success.

Another huge benefit of the nutrition plan I propose is my clients start to feel happy. And why is that? After all, I am a Health Coach and not the "Happiness Coach." It's a combination of both physiology and a positive mindset. As to the physiology part, neurotransmitters are made in the gut and my clients have healed their guts—a healed gut means more neurotransmitters such as serotonin and dopamine, which make you feel good and motivated. This alone can be life-changing.

Now, while it is simple, like anything else new, it may not be easy...*at first*. Once you get your pantry and refrigerator set up, become accustomed to different ingredients, and learn to cook whole foods instead of using processed foods, you'll feel better and see results. This will motivate you to keep going.

What is this diet?

Let's get rid of the word *diet* and call it a nutrition plan, or better yet, a nutrition lifestyle!

And what is this nutrient-dense, blood-sugar balancing, anti-inflammatory, gut-healing nutrition lifestyle all about?

I'll start with what it does include:

- Vegetables
- Fruits

- Beef, chicken, turkey, pork, eggs, bacon, bison, seafood (shrimp, salmon, cod, etc.)
- Nuts, nut butters, and seeds
- Seasonings

Foods not included:

- Sugar
- Industrial vegetable/seed oils (top offenders are soybean, canola, and corn oil)
- Grains (including oatmeal)
- Legumes (including peanuts/peanut butter)
- Dairy
- Alcohol (don't shoot the messenger!)

Don't let this "to be avoided" list scare you. Except for sugar and the industrial vegetable/seed oils, these food groups may be individually reintroduced later when your goals have been met, and it's a good idea to monitor your body's response.

But let's get into a bit more about the "to be avoided" foods now. When you understand why these are being removed, you are more likely to adhere to the plan.

Sugar

Refined sugar is problematic. Here's what it does:

- It interferes with hormones, leading to insulin and fat-storage issues.
- It accelerates aging.

- It is inflammatory (the root cause of many diseases).
- It interferes with the immune system.

In short, sugar is *unhealthy*.

Avoiding sugar is one of the best things you can do to help meet your health goals and avoid health issues.

And sugar cravings and addiction are real things. Flooding your body with nutritious foods can be helpful here. Replacing refined-sugar foods with healthy foods is an adjustment, a job in itself—this is not the time to calorie-count. Calories do matter, but they're not the priority when you're going through a sugar-removal process.

Because sugar is physically addictive, your body will go through a withdrawal process. As well, sugar gives you "dopamine hits" when you're feeling low, stressed, or tired. Withdrawal symptoms you may experience include headaches, fatigue, mood changes, body pain, or some combination of these.

Tips to help you adjust through this process are coming up, but first, what about natural sweeteners?

Honey and maple syrup are the top options here, but I recommend limiting or avoiding them completely until you've met your goals. Runners-up are coconut sugar and date sugar. However, these sweeteners are still glucose-rich and it's best to limit or avoid them altogether until you've met your health goals. Once you have, natural sweeteners should still be consumed in moderation, such as in the 20% of an 80/20 nutrition approach in which 80% of the time you're in full compliance with healthy nutrition (and lifestyle habits) and 20% of the time you can veer off to some extent.

What about zero-calorie sweeteners? Some are good options and others not.

- Zero-calorie natural sweeteners such as stevia and monk fruit are preferred options (such as stevia in coffee or tea).
- Erythritol is a popular zero-calorie sweetener. Technically, this is "natural" sweetener, but it can cause digestive issues for some, interfering with nutrient absorption, and I recommend avoiding it completely until you've met your health and weight-loss goals, then add it back in and monitor for any symptoms.
- Zero-calorie sweeteners to avoid are sucralose, aspartame, and saccharin. These are non-natural artificial sweeteners and can interfere with the gut microbiome (which in turn can interfere with achieving your health goals).

The following can help to get through the sugar-elimination process:

- Have healthy fats with meals and snacks. Healthy fats such as nuts, nut butter, avocado, coconut butter, butter, and mayonnaise help to satiate you and thus help reduce the cravings. As well, fats can help mitigate the blood glucose/insulin response to carbohydrates which can help cravings.
  - Snack options such as apples with nut butter, beef sticks, turkey sticks, hard boiled eggs, deviled eggs, guacamole with sliced bell peppers, olives, nuts/seeds, and pickles rolled up with a quality turkey lunchmeat can be helpful.
- L-glutamine is a supplement that may be helpful for sugar cravings (and helps with gut health).

○ You can take L-glutamine as a capsule that you swallow like any other supplement taken orally, or you can sprinkle it directly into your mouth when you have a sugar craving.

○ According to the Naturally Nourished podcast,

"[L-glutamine] does play a role with our blood-sugar regulation and blood-sugar cravings, and addictive impulse activity is tied to glutamine depletion. So L-glutamine has been used to recover in rehab centers, to be taken sublingually, like just a direct scoop under the tongue to help with cravings and impulse activity."

○ If you decide to take L-glutamine as a sprinkle under your tongue, check with the supplement manufacturer to confirm that it is safe to do so. There may be certain fillers in it that contraindicate that route.

○ If you're interested in L-glutamine for sugar cravings, be sure to get approval from your doctor before starting it.

○ If you do opt to get it, see "Appendix C" for recommended brands.

● Stay properly hydrated with water (more on water later), and adding electrolytes may be helpful (see "Appendix C" for quality brands, but as with any other supplement, get your doctor's approval before starting electrolytes).

Industrial Vegetable and Seed Oils

Next up are industrial vegetable and seed oils.

This topic can be difficult because these inferior oils are rampant in processed foods.

"Industrial" (or "refined") oils include oils such as soybean, canola, corn, cottonseed, sunflower, and safflower oil. These oils are very unhealthy as they are highly inflammatory. And most, if not all, medical professionals, including conventional practitioners, agree that inflammation is a contributing factor in many health issues.

Industrial oils are bad because they oxidize to form free radicals that can cause damage to cell membranes in the body. Over time, the damage can cause premature aging (and we're not talking just aesthetics here), heart disease, obesity, and inflammation.

Refined industrial vegetable/seed oils are so unstable that they can start to oxidize when exposed to air, light, or moisture. What's worse is when these oils are heated, further free-radical damage occurs.

According to **www.dsengineers.com**, the main steps for the edible-oil refining process are:

1. Degumming
2. Neutralizing
3. Bleaching
4. Deodorizing
5. Winterizing
6. Fractionation
7. Hydrogenation
8. Interesterification

No wonder our bodies don't respond favorably to these oils!

So, if industrial vegetable/seed oils are eliminated, which oils are stable for cooking?

These would be temperature-stable saturated fats that will not oxidize, such as coconut oil, butter, ghee (clarified butter), and saturated animal fats (lard, tallow). Avocado oil is a great option for cooking, as well.

- Extra virgin olive oil has a lower smoke point, so it's not the best for cooking at higher temperatures (it may turn into an inflammatory oil!). To be on the safe side, I don't recommend using olive oil at all for cooking. Instead, add it to cooked foods when they have been removed from the heat.

- Note that olive oil is an excellent healthy fat choice in salad dressings, or drizzled onto cooked vegetables after they have been taken off the heat source.

A word of caution regarding salad dressings and mayonnaise:

Most conventional salad dressings need to be avoided due to the industrial vegetable/seed oils they contain. Read the labels: even if the front label specifies "made with olive oil" or "made with avocado oil," turn the jar around and read those ingredients. Oftentimes other oils such as soybean oil are used in combination with the healthy oils, making these a bad choice.

Any homemade dressing you make with the right oils will be good. Easy homemade salad dressings can be made with:

- Olive oil and lemon juice
- Olive oil and balsamic vinegar, apple cider vinegar, or red wine vinegar
- Lemon juice with ripened smashed avocado
- You can sprinkle on basil, oregano, and salt for additional flavoring.

"Primal Kitchen" is a quality brand for salad dressings, but note some may have dairy (be sure to review the ingredients while doing a dairy-elimination reset). Note that at the time of this writing, I am not being paid by Primal Kitchen products for the shout-out here, but I do recommend them.

Most conventional mayonnaise brands have industrial vegetable/seed oils in them, as well.

Quality brands made with avocado oil include "Primal Kitchen" and "Sir Kensington." I have seen these in conventional grocery stores.

Another option is to make homemade mayonnaise. There are many recipes online for homemade versions.

Note that when you go out to eat, it is very difficult or close to impossible to be "industrial vegetable/seed oil" free. To get the most out of this 28-day plan, limit or avoid going out to eat.

When you've met your health goals, going out to eat and being exposed to these inferior oils can be the 20% in your 80/20 lifestyle (but be sure to keep them out of your house!). Do your best here.

Grains

Let's go against the grain here next. That's right, grains are next on the "to be avoided" food categories list.

Grains include wheat, corn, rice, pasta, cereals, barley, millet, rye, oats/oatmeal, etc.

We're eliminating grains during this kickstart for several reasons—this includes eliminating "whole grains," too. But before going into the reasons for eliminating grains, note that removing 100% grains is not necessarily forever, and some grains are better choices than others (such as quinoa, rice, and gluten-free oatmeal). As well, when you've met your health goals, including the better grain options in the 20% of your 80/20 lifestyle is fine, provided you tolerate them well.

So why eliminate grains?

Grains do not have a high nutritional value. They contain antinutrients that can interfere with digestion (decreasing vitamin and mineral absorption) and can be inflammatory. As well, they can cause a strong blood glucose and insulin response, which is unhelpful for attaining health goals.

What are the antinutrients found in grains?

- **Lectins:** These are natural plant toxins that can cause damage to the intestinal lining. This can allow foreign proteins to enter the bloodstream and prompt an autoimmune response (we're talking about inflammation here, too).

- **Gluten:** This also can cause damage to the intestinal lining and thereby an inflammatory response. The response can be very individual and even if you don't have celiac disease, you can still be negatively affected by gluten.
  - A note about wheat: it is "double-sprayed" with glyphosate (a herbicide)—during growth and at harvest to prevent mold. Glyphosate alone can be very problematic.

- **Phytates:** These can block nutrient absorption. There are some nutritional benefits when they're consumed in moderation, but too much can lead to nutrient deficiencies.

Removing grains for a period of time can help heal the gut, which in turn can help you to get to your health goals.

A note about processed gluten-free products: These are not a great option when you're working toward your health goals. They are processed and may interfere with blood-glucose balance, which in turn will interfere with your health goals. More on insulin and why this matters will be addressed in a later chapter.

The same applies to goods made with "gluten-free" flours. While these are a better choice, the foods made with them can still have a higher "carb load" and interfere with blood-glucose balance. Nevertheless, goods made with gluten-free flours are better options in the 20% of living an 80/20 lifestyle when your goals are met than are wheat or other "non" gluten-free flours.

For grain-free meal ideas, check out the recipes in "Appendix A."

Legumes

Up next are legumes. This category mainly includes beans and peanuts (and the beloved peanut butter).

Legumes are actually less problematic than grains. This is because they have a higher nutritional value and lower levels of lectins and phytates (antinutrients). However, the antinutrients they do contain can cause digestive symptoms. Part of the 28-Day Kickstart Plan is to heal the gut, and avoiding potentially problematic foods for a period of time can help you get to your health goals.

And regarding the fiber found in beans, you can get ample fiber from vegetables and fruits. A diet heavy in grains and legumes can easily deliver excess fiber that may lead to constipation, inhibited nutrient absorption, and other digestive problems.

The protein-to-carbohydrate ratio in beans is not ideal either. More on protein and carbohydrate impact on insulin balance will be addressed in later chapters.

I'm generally fine with beans being a part of a healthy nutrition plan provided it has been determined that these are not problematic for the individual (after an elimination period such as this 28-Day Kickstart Plan and monitoring for symptoms when reintroduced) *and* they are part of the 20% of an 80/20 lifestyle when goals have been met.

Dairy

This one can be difficult, but I assure you, the benefits of eliminating dairy for a period of time are worth it.

For many people, dairy can be an inflammatory food. The casein protein in dairy can be the culprit here.

Note that dairy does have some great nutrition, but it's worthwhile to find out if you have any individual tolerance issues with it. Going 100% dairy-free for 30 days is recommended as a reset. After a 30-day dairy-free reset, check in on how you feel. If your symptoms have improved, consider going dairy-free longer. However, if you would like to add dairy back into your diet, I recommend implementing a staged approach for reintroducing dairy. (Note that eggs are not dairy.)

After each dairy type has been added in, monitor for symptoms such as:

- Fatigue
- Joint pain
- Increased intensity of existing pain

- New pain anywhere on the body
- Headache
- Skin issues
- Nasal congestion
- Cough
- Brain fog
- Puffiness anywhere on the body
- Increased blood pressure
- Weight gain
- Digestive issues
- Increased intensity of existing digestive issues
- Feeling "off" in any way

Note: You may not experience symptoms for up to 72 hours after the reintroduction. I recommend not adding a new dairy type for one week in between each new type added.

If you experience any of the symptoms listed above, the dairy type that has been reintroduced may be a problematic food for you. You may need either to avoid it or to heal your gut before adding it again.

Some people can tolerate certain dairy types over others. It can be very individual.

This is the recommended staged approach for reintroducing dairy:

- Start first with butter (or ghee, which is also known as clarified butter) and monitor for the symptoms listed above. Do not add any other dairy types for one week. Butter is first because it has trace amounts of casein and may be better tolerated for that reason. Note that ghee/clarified butter has had the casein removed. If butter is problematic, try ghee.

- If adding butter is successful for a week (no symptoms), the next dairy product to add is hard cheese (such as cheddar or Parmesan). The enzymes formed in the aging process for hard cheese make it easier to digest ("friendlier" for your digestive system), so this is a good choice to add next.

- After hard cheese, try yogurt (plain full-fat unsweetened yogurt is best with fresh/frozen fruit added as desired), then heavy cream, then other types such as cream cheese, sour cream, etc.

- After heavy cream, dairy types to be reintroduced are based on your preference. You can skip yogurt and heavy cream if you don't care for either. Yogurt and heavy cream are added after hard cheese because these tend to be better tolerated.

- Give each new dairy type a week before adding the new one. Monitor for the above-mentioned symptoms after each type is introduced.

- Some people do very well with raw milk products or goat, sheep, and camel milk products, but not cow milk products. If you are having issues with the cow milk options, try these out. This is very individual.

- Note that some people cannot go past butter and hard cheese without symptoms (because these tend to be better tolerated dairy sources).

And the question I often get after talking about a dairy elimination is "what about calcium?" This is a great question. It's important for women to include foods with calcium in their nutrition plan, but it's possible to do this without dairy.

Here are some dairy-free calcium sources to get you started. There are some uncommon vegetables listed and I invite you to explore some of these options (toss in a salad or soup!).

Vegetables	Other
Beet greens	Almonds
Bok choy	Almond butter
Broccoli	Beans (cooked black, garbanzo, pinto, white)
Broccoli rabe	Canned salmon (w/edible bones)
Butternut squash	Canned sardines (w/edible bones)
Collard greens	Chia seeds
Kale	Dried figs
Mustard greens	Eggs
Okra	Oranges
Spinach	Sesame seeds
Sweet potatoes	Shrimp
Turnip greens	Sunflower seeds

Be careful with store-bought nut milks (almond, hazelnut, macadamia, cashew) as they are often fortified with calcium. (The added calcium may be of a lower quality and so may not be absorbed well.) It's best to have the almonds or almond butter in the whole, natural form.

Another question I get often is regarding what can be used to replace coffee creamer when dairy is eliminated. You can use unsweetened nut milk or unsweetened coconut milk. Another option is to use vanilla (or chocolate) collagen peptide powders to help flavor your coffee (these have the added bonus of protein).

- A word of caution: If you're prone to kidney stones, avoid collagen peptide powders.

While it's not my top choice for creamer, check out the Nutpods brand if these options are not working out well for you. Avoid their oat milk versions (because you will be grain-free for the kickstart). Stick with the coconut and almond versions.

- This brand does have some "gums" in the ingredients (such as gellan gum); these are not ideal but okay to use as an alternative. However, if you experience a "stall" in your progress, revisit using Nutpods for creamer, as the gum may be causing an issue. I have some clients using this brand who are having excellent progress while others have stalls. This is very individual.

For dairy-free yogurt options, try unsweetened coconut or almond yogurt. Cocojune is a popular brand of coconut yogurt. But watch out for sweeteners in the dairy-free yogurts because you are avoiding sugar in this plan. Add in fresh or frozen fruit to sweeten it naturally.

Alcohol

Alcohol is next up. There are differing views regarding alcohol from a health standpoint. You can find supporting studies on both sides of the fence. But at the end of the day, your liver deals with alcohol as a toxin. If you have a meal with alcohol, the first thing your liver will tend to is the alcohol.

I recommend avoiding alcohol completely while completing the 28-Day Kickstart Plan. If you do opt to have alcohol during the plan, I recommend that you reduce the amount by 50% or more and consume it only one or two days a week. And if you do have it, have gluten-free, sugar-free versions (no beer, no sugary mixed drinks!) and have wine (red is best) or a hard liquor such as tequila with lime and seltzer water.

But again, zero is best for this plan. Consuming alcohol will slow your progress toward meeting your health goals. Alcohol may even stall progress altogether for some!

Going Out

What about when you're going to a social gathering or out to a restaurant?

I get this question a lot. When attending a family or social gathering, bring a dish. You'll find you need to bring an ample amount, as people find these foods delicious. And for desserts, fruit is your friend.

For eating out at restaurants, if possible, check the menu online before visiting the restaurant to get an idea of the available options. Also, keep in mind that it can be difficult or next to impossible to avoid industrial vegetable and seed oils, but do your best with everything else.

Here are some guidelines to help with restaurant options:

- **Grilled or roasted meats:** Look for dishes that feature high-quality protein sources like steak, chicken, pork, or fish. Avoid breaded or fried options, and opt for simple grilled or roasted preparations. If a dish is prepared with a marinade or sauce, be sure to ask what the ingredients are, or better yet, ask them to prepare it without them. For burgers, get a bunless version.

- **Salads:** Choose salads with fresh vegetables, mixed greens, and a protein source such as grilled chicken or shrimp. Ask for oil and vinegar and/or lemon wedges as a dressing, or try some salsa or guacamole on your salad. The oils in restaurants will most likely be made with industrial vegetable and seed oils and this is a matter of "just do your best." And skip the croutons!

- **Vegetable sides:** Many restaurants offer vegetable side dishes such as steamed or roasted broccoli, Brussels sprouts, or asparagus. These can be great options to accompany your main course.

- **Eggs:** Omelets or scrambled eggs with vegetables and meat can be suitable choices for breakfast or brunch. A word of caution concerning omelets and scrambled eggs—many restaurants add pancake or wheat flour to the egg mixture to make them fluffier. Be sure to ask about this and if they do, ask them to omit it, or order your eggs sunny-side up, over easy, basted, or poached instead.

- **Soups:** Avoid soups! These are typically not healthy in restaurants. Substitute a side of fruit instead or salad instead.

- **Guacamole or salsa:** These can be good options for appetizers or condiments to accompany your main dish.

- If getting potatoes, avoid french fries, hash browns, and American fries. Opt for baked potatoes and request that these be served plain (you can salt them). Note that baked sweet potatoes are a great choice (and you can request that cinnamon be sprinkled on them if you like).

- Order double protein servings!

CHAPTER 9

꧁❀꧂

HYDRATE FOR HEALTH

*H*ave you ever thought about how an act as simple as drinking water can do wonders for your health? It's true! Water is one of the most effective and accessible routes to improving your overall well-being. Let's dive into the numerous benefits of staying hydrated:

1. **Helps with weight loss:** If shedding a few pounds is on your agenda, water can be your ally. Drinking an adequate amount of water can help you feel full and satisfied, reducing the temptation to overeat.

2. **Boosts energy:** Say goodbye to that midday slump! Proper hydration revitalizes your body and mind, keeping you energized and focused throughout the day.

3. **Improves mood:** Feeling a bit down? Water might just lift your spirits. Staying hydrated supports your brain function, which can positively influence your mood.

4. **Enhances focus and cognition:** Need a mental boost? Hydration can improve your cognitive function, making it

easier to think clearly and stay sharp. (Fun fact: Your brain is made up of about 73% water.)

5. **Promotes skin health:** Forget expensive skin-care products; water is nature's best gift for your skin. Hydration keeps your skin glowing, moisturized, and less prone to a number of issues including dryness.

6. **Supports digestion and detoxification:** Your immune system will love you for this. Drinking enough water aids in digestion and helps your body flush out toxins effectively.

Inadequate hydration, on the other hand, can lead to a host of problems—from reduced brain power to increased fatigue. So, it's time to give water the attention it deserves!

Our bodies are remarkable, composed of about 60% water. Yet, many people drink barely enough water to sustain themselves properly. Instead, they consume sugary coffee in the morning, soda or other sweetened beverages with lunch, and perhaps alcohol or more soda in the evening.

However, relying on these calorie-heavy drinks contributes to another problem: even with all those liquid calories, people often still feel hungry. It's a vicious cycle that keeps them reaching for more processed, sugary, and unhealthy foods.

But fear not! I have a simple solution to help you feel better and reach your health goals—ditch the calorie-heavy drinks and embrace beverages with one or two natural ingredients. For instance, water with a refreshing squeeze of lemon can be both healthy and satisfying.

Speaking of water, let me emphasize it once again: drink more water! Your body will thank you for it.

Here's more of what you need to know about beverages:

Soda is perhaps the worst thing you can put in your body because it contains a couple of destructive ingredients, most dominantly high-fructose corn syrup. However, diet drinks aren't much better, because your body reacts to the chemicals added as if the soda contained sugar, even when it technically doesn't. Drinking diet drinks rarely leads to losing weight; in fact, it dulls your taste response so you need more and more processed, sugary, and unhealthy foods in order to enjoy them as much.

By cutting out diet drinks, you will slowly start to enjoy eating healthier food because you'll regain your full taste-bud function over time.

Avoid soda at all costs. If soda is something really important to you, try taking the next 30 days off. You'll find your taste buds will likely not enjoy it as much when you taste it again.

Generally, drinking a total of half of your weight in ounces of water is a minimum requirement. For health goals, a goal is to drink 100–128 ounces a day. If you are a petite person (under 5 feet, 4 inches tall), your water requirements may be less.

As a starting point for everyone, I recommend measuring your water intake for a couple days to confirm how much you are actually drinking. If you're drinking less than 75 ounces a day, incrementally increase to 75 ounces a day as a first goal.

- When you meet 75 ounces a day, incrementally increase until you meet the goal of 100 ounces a day.

- It's important to increase gradually so the body can adjust.
  - This is especially true when you cut out sugar and high/fast-burning carbohydrate foods (grains) in your nutrition plan, which is what you will be doing here. When you reduce carbohydrate intake, your body begins to process electrolytes differently. This is because your insulin level will be lower and when this happens, your kidneys excrete more sodium. Sodium is balanced with other electrolytes, so the loss of sodium may cause imbalances in other electrolytes, as well.
  - In addition, you may need more salt and/or electrolytes in your diet as you increase water intake and this can help with your body's adjustment to increased water.
    - For salt, use a high-quality version such as Redmond Real Salt brand, Sea Salt, or Himalayan salt.
    - If you do add electrolytes, use a quality brand as listed in "Appendix C" and get your licensed health-care practitioner's approval before starting them. And no, Gatorade is not a good option!
  - If you feel dizzy, get leg cramps, or feel "off," or it interferes with your sleep, then back down to the prior amount you were drinking (your body hasn't adjusted yet).

Water-Drinking Tips

- Using stainless steel or glass water bottles with measurements is a great way to track your water. Or place a pitcher of water in your refrigerator every morning with the required amount.

- You can flavor your water by infusing it with produce. Add slices of lemons, limes, cucumber, oranges, or strawberries. A word of caution regarding your tooth enamel and citrus: It's best to drink with a straw or rinse out your mouth after drinking to protect the enamel.

- I'm often asked about sparkling water or other versions of water. Spring water (Mountain Valley brand), filtered water, and bottled mineral water (such as San Pellegrino or Perrier) are excellent water sources. If you can access spring water, that is the best.

- If you'd like reminders to drink water throughout the day, there are free daily water tracking apps available. Google "track my water app" to see the different options.

Now that you know the importance of staying hydrated, it's time to prioritize your daily water intake. Your body will thank you, and you'll be well on your way to improved health and well-being. Cheers to a healthier, more hydrated you!

CHAPTER 10

⚜

FERTILIZER FOR FAT CELLS

*W*hat on earth is fertilizer for fat cells? That would be insulin.

Now, before you get alarmed, let's clear something up: insulin is essential for your survival. You can't live without it. However, like many things in life, balance is key, and that's what we'll explore here.

Understanding Insulin

Insulin plays a crucial role in your body. Its primary job is to regulate blood-glucose levels by helping to transport sugar from your bloodstream into cells, where it can be used as an energy source. This hormone also aids in storing excess glucose as glycogen in your liver and muscles. When those glycogen stores are full, any leftover glucose gets converted into fat and stored in adipose tissue.

Imbalanced Insulin

Problems arise when we have an imbalance in insulin levels, particularly due to an overabundance of carbohydrates, especially those "fast" burning ones like those in products loaded with refined sugar. These can cause what we call "insulin spikes," which act as fertilizer for your fat cells, promoting fat storage rather than burning it for energy.

Having a focus on "smart carbs" is helpful. Smart carbohydrates are vegetables and fruits.

That said, even though vegetables and fruits are great carbohydrate options, these still turn into glucose in your body, which in turn, causes insulin to be secreted. You do want this to happen! To help mitigate the "blood glucose-insulin" response—to slow it down—have healthy fats with carbohydrates. We are talking about avocados (hello guacamole!), coconut products (unsweetened coconut flakes/chips, coconut butter, unsweetened coconut yogurt, coconut oil, MCT oil), nuts/seeds, nut/seed butter, olives, and eggs. (Grass-fed butter can also be a great healthy fat option, but it is dairy and is omitted as part of the reset process in this plan.)

Also, it's important to note that insulin sensitivity decreases in menopause and beyond. What this means is you are moving toward being insulin-resistant. When your cells become resistant to insulin, this leads to elevated blood-glucose levels, which can lead to weight gain, prediabetes, and type 2 diabetes. Also, losing weight becomes more difficult because the excess blood glucose is being stored as fat.

The "calories in/calories out is the bottom line for weight loss" philosophy is blown out of the water when it comes to insulin resistance. It's difficult to lose weight while in a state of insulin resistance—and not a good idea to keep dropping calories consumed. Your body needs nutrition!

I must mention that even healthy versions of carbohydrates consumed in excess are not a good idea. For example, sometimes on my intake calls with new clients, they will proudly tell me about how they eat delicious healthy smoothies daily. When asked what their smoothies include, they tell me they are all-fruit smoothies. But without healthy fat and protein in there, this is a metabolic disaster! Delicious? Absolutely. Is fruit nutritious? Absolutely. But not in excess like this and not without healthy fat along for the ride.

I'm a fan of fruit. But while working toward your health goals, I recommend focusing on "low-glycemic" (or lower-"sugar") fruits such as berries (blueberries, strawberries, blackberries, raspberries), grapefruit, lemons, limes, and green apples until you reach your goals. You can enjoy other fruits, but have them on a limited basis until you reach your goals. And even when you reach your goals, I recommend that you continue to focus on these fruits to some extent because they are loaded with great nutrition and will be better for your overall blood glucose balance.

Go ahead and have that delicious watermelon in summer or red apples in the fall—just don't have them daily when you're work-ing toward your goals. And when you meet your goals, enjoy the higher-sugar fruits, but be sure to mix in some of the lower-sugar fruits regularly.

When it comes to how much fruit to consume, I generally recom-mend having three servings of vegetables to every one serving of fruit on a given day as the goal and having a "two-to-one" ratio as a minimum. The "three-to-one" ratio is best for optimal health results.

A word about zero-calorie sweeteners:

- These may cause an insulin response due to a brain func-tion that occurs when your tongue tastes the sweetener, but note that this response can be individual. This does include stevia and monk fruit.

- If you are using zero-calorie sweeteners, including stevia or monk fruit, and are experiencing a stall in your progress, reduce the amount or avoid altogether until you've met your goals. After you have, reintroduce them and monitor for response. This can be very individual.

- Note that artificial zero-calorie sweeteners (sucralose, aspartame, saccharin) can disrupt your microbiome—and when your microbiome is disrupted, the path to your health goals is disrupted.

Remember, finding the right balance with insulin is essential for your overall well-being. Be mindful of your carbohydrate choices, embrace healthy fats, and stay on track to a healthier you!

~oﬂo~

PROTEIN FOR THE WIN!

*L*et's unravel the importance of protein. Protein is a vital nutrient that offers a multitude of benefits and needs to be a star player in your daily nutrition plan.

The Power of Protein

Protein is a true powerhouse. It's not only satiating, keeping you fuller for longer, but it also boosts your metabolism and plays a crucial role in building and maintaining muscle. As you age, the need for protein becomes even more pronounced, especially for women in midlife and beyond. With aging, stomach-acid function becomes less efficient, leading to impaired protein digestion and absorption. So, it's essential to increase your protein intake to ensure adequate absorption, which in turn supports muscle, strength, bone health, and other vital body functions.

Bridge the Protein Gap

You might be surprised to learn that many women don't consume enough protein in their diets. By increasing your protein intake, you'll be taking a significant step toward achieving your health goals, particularly in weight loss and muscle maintenance.

The Muscle Connection

Maintaining good muscle mass as you age can significantly affect how well you age overall. Preserving muscle is of the utmost importance. You definitely don't want to lose muscle as the years go by.

Muscle expert Dr. Gabrielle Lyon highlights the link between muscle health and longevity. On her website (www.drgabrielle-lyon.com), she emphasizes that more muscle means less fragility, fewer falls, increased strength, and better mobility. With ample muscle mass, you're better equipped to fight off illnesses, recover from injuries, maintain cognitive abilities, and even prevent chronic diseases.

The Magic of Protein with Strength and Resistance Training

To preserve and grow muscle, a combination of ample protein intake and strength or resistance training is the winning formula. We'll delve into resistance and strength training in detail in an upcoming chapter, but for now, let's focus on the importance of protein.

Improved Insulin Sensitivity

Maintaining muscle mass does more than just help you stay strong; it also improves insulin sensitivity. As mentioned in the previous chapter, insulin sensitivity tends to decrease with age, making it crucial to optimize it for overall health.

Protein Goals for Midlife Women

For women in midlife and beyond, aiming for 90–100 grams of protein a day (by nutrition grams, not weight grams) is vital. Unless your doctor prescribes a lower protein requirement for medical reasons, sticking to this target is a wise move.

To ensure you're meeting your protein needs, aim for a minimum of 30 grams of protein at each meal. There are plenty of delicious foods that can help you achieve this goal:

- **Chicken breast:** A 4-ounce (113 grams) serving of cooked chicken breast contains roughly 35 grams of protein.

- **Turkey breast:** Similar to chicken breast, a 4-ounce (113 grams) serving of cooked turkey breast provides around 34 grams of protein.

- **Ground turkey 93/7 (93% lean/7% fat):** A 5-ounce (142 grams) serving provides approximately 28 grams of protein, and a 6-ounce (170 grams) serving has approximately 34 grams of protein.

- **Ground chicken:** A 4-ounce (113 grams) serving of ground chicken provides around 27 grams of protein, and a 5-ounce (142 grams) serving provides 33 grams of protein.

- **Lean beef:** A 4-ounce (113 grams) serving of lean beef, such as sirloin or tenderloin, contains approximately 28–30 grams of protein.

- **Pork tenderloin:** A 4-ounce (113 grams) serving of cooked pork tenderloin offers roughly 29 grams of protein.

- **Fish:** Different types of fish vary in their protein content. For example, a 4-ounce (113 grams) serving of salmon provides around 25 grams of protein, while tuna can offer about 30 grams of protein per 4-ounce serving.

- **Eggs:** Two large eggs provide roughly 12–14 grams of protein. To meet the 30-gram goal, you could have 4–5 eggs.

- **Greek yogurt:** A cup (240 grams) of plain Greek yogurt typically contains around 20 grams of protein. You could have 1.5 cups to reach the 30-gram mark.

  - While the kickstart involves being dairy-free, when dairy is reintroduced and it has been determined that you don't have any issues with yogurt, this is a great protein option (the unsweetened version, of course). You can add fresh fruit for natural sweetening.

If getting more protein into your daily nutrition plan is challenging, you can add one protein smoothie a day. This is a great way to add more protein. However, I don't recommend that all of your protein be consumed as smoothies. This should be in addition to consuming whole food protein sources.

A big plus of incorporating protein smoothies in your nutrition plan is that you can get *a lot* of nutrition from them when they're also loaded with greens and healthy fats such as avocados. But please don't make your protein smoothie "fruit heavy"; your blood-sugar level will thank you. You'll find balanced protein smoothie recipes in "Appendix A."

Here are a few other tips for protein smoothies:

- When making a protein smoothie, in addition to the protein powder, be sure to include healthy fats and carbohydrates (healthy fats include: unsweetened coconut milk/ coconut cream, unsweetened coconut yogurt, MCT oil if tolerated, coconut oil, coconut butter, avocado, nut butters, and chia seeds).

- o Be sure to include a healthy fat to help mitigate the blood-sugar response from the rapid digestion of it.

- o Be sure to include more veggies than fruit (such as 1½ cups of spinach and ½ cup of berries).

- o Avoid having a "fruit only" or "mainly fruit" smoothie to avoid blood-sugar issues (blood-sugar imbalances are not helpful with meeting health and weight loss goals).

My recommended protein powder type is beef protein. You'll find some recommendations in "Appendix C."

I generally do not recommend whey protein powders, mainly because they can be a source of inflammation (dairy is the culprit). Also, you should avoid whey protein powder if you have an auto-immune condition and are following the Autoimmune Protocol nutrition plan (also known as "AIP").

I also generally don't recommend plant-based protein powders (such as rice, soy, and pea) because the protein absorption may be questionable and these can be inflammatory, especially for those with autoimmune conditions.

However, if you are compelled to get a plant-based protein powder, then pea protein is the best option, as it contains a better balance of essential amino acids than do the other options.

If quality beef protein powders are cost-prohibitive, you can use collagen peptide powders; these tend to be less expensive. But I would like to mention a few things about collagen peptide powders here.

- Collagen peptide powders differ from beef protein powders. Collagen can be great for a healthy gut, joints, skin, and hair—but it's not a complete protein. It's missing the amino acid tryptophan. However, note that collagen peptide powders still count toward your protein macros in food tracking apps.

- While collagen peptide powders can be part of a healthy diet, these should not be your only source of protein since they are incomplete.
    - Some collagen supplements/powders may be fortified with tryptophan, but that involves a high level of processing, which interferes with the amino acid properties.
    - A word of caution: If you have a history of kidney stones (calcium oxalate stones), it's best to avoid collagen supplements and peptide powders because they can metabolize to oxalates. If you've suffered from kidney stones, you likely already know all about oxalates!

I often get asked if beans, rice, or quinoa (plant proteins) are good protein sources. The big issue here is that you need to eat a lot of them to get a sufficient amount of protein. As Dr. Gabrielle Lyon points out, plant protein and animal protein are not equal. It takes six cups of quinoa to get the same amino acid profile as four ounces of chicken, and the calorie difference is huge. That's a lot of quinoa! And this is a significant carbohydrate load (remember the prior chapter about insulin balance). So, while it's not impossible to meet protein and amino acid requirements when consuming solely plant-based protein, you'll need to eat a lot of it and your calories will definitely be increased. Calories do matter; they are just not the only driver for meeting weight loss goals, especially for women in midlife and beyond.

CHAPTER 12

INTERMITTENT FASTING: DON'T WORRY, YOU WON'T STARVE!

*N*ow we'll delve into the world of Intermittent Fasting (IF). This eating pattern has become a powerful tool for improving health on multiple levels, and my hope is that you'll not only try it during the 28-Day Kickstart Plan, but also adopt it as a sustainable lifestyle for ongoing benefits.

What Is Intermittent Fasting?

IF is an eating pattern that cycles between periods of fasting and eating. It's not a new concept; fasting has been practiced for centuries, often for religious or spiritual reasons, in Islam, Christianity, Judaism, Buddhism, and other faiths.

Who Is IF For?

IF is for anyone who wants to improve their health. It's a convenient, easy-to-follow, and sustainable way to enhance overall well-being.

Who Isn't IF For?

There are a few groups for whom IF isn't recommended, such as pregnant and nursing moms, children, and those who are severely underweight or have eating disorders.

A Word of Caution

If you're taking medications for diabetes, it's essential to work closely with your doctor while doing IF. Consider using a Continuous Glucose Monitor for valuable data during this period.

The Benefits of IF

Intermittent Fasting allows your body to undergo a process called autophagy, in which old and damaged cells are cleared out, leaving room for new cells to thrive. Autophagy brings an array of benefits, including reduced inflammation, an enhanced immune system, improved skin health (anti-aging effects!), increased generation of brain cells, and better memory, mood, and focus. It's truly a remarkable process with an array of positive impacts.

Other benefits of IF include:

- Enhancement of brain-derived neurotrophic factor (BDNF), helping the brain manage stress
- Easing of depression
- Facilitation of weight loss
- Reduction of cortisol levels (the stress hormone)
- Promotion of good sleep
- Support for detoxification
- Improvement of insulin sensitivity (especially important as insulin sensitivity decreases in menopause and beyond)

- Significant increase in Human Growth Hormone (HGH) levels, which aids in fat loss, muscle gain, sugar metabolism, and fat metabolism

Different Fasting Timelines

There are several IF schedules you can follow. Two popular examples are the "16:8" cycle, with a 16-hour fasting period and an 8-hour eating window, and the occasional implementation of a 24-hour fast.

Starting with 12-Hour Fasting

For beginners, I recommend starting with a 12-hour fasting window and a 12-hour eating window. If that feels challenging, you can begin with a shorter fasting window and gradually increase it by one hour each week until you reach a daily 16-hour fasting window.

Enhancing Your Fasting Experience

To boost the benefits of fasting, you can add either one 24-hour fast or one 20-hour fast each week. However, even if you follow a daily 16:8 plan without these extended fasts, you'll still experience significant benefits.

Calorie Timing, Not Restriction

IF is more about "calorie timing" than "calorie restriction." It won't slow down your metabolism—that occurs with calorie restriction, not calorie timing. In fact, some studies suggest that short periods of fasting may increase metabolism.

What to Drink During the Fast

You can enjoy the following during your fasting window:

- Water
- Water with unsweetened electrolytes

- Black coffee (unsweetened, no cream)
- Tea (unsweetened, no cream)

Steer Clear of "Dirty Fasting"

Stevia, monk fruit, BCAAs, and collagen peptide powders will technically break your fast and are referred to as dirty fasting. I don't recommend including these during your fasting period, as they may stall your progress.

Breaking Your Fast

Breaking a 16:8 fast or shorter periods typically doesn't cause significant digestive symptoms. However, for longer fasts, the digestive system needs a gentle "wake-up." To be on the safe side, avoid nuts, seeds, and raw vegetables as your first meal. Eggs and raw vegetables may cause symptoms for some, so listen to your body and adjust accordingly.

A Pre-Meal Option

If you experience digestive symptoms after breaking a longer fast, consider having a "pre-meal" 30 minutes prior to your regular first meal. Include a small serving of avocado or cooked foods such as fish, beef, or vegetables. Avoid raw vegetables and nuts/seeds with the pre-meal.

The Magic of IF

Intermittent Fasting is a vast topic, and if you wish to dive deeper, check out "Appendix C" for recommendations. I encourage you to embrace IF as a lifestyle, watch the magic happen, and experience the profound benefits it brings to your overall health and well-being.

CHAPTER 13

꧁꧂

LET'S GET PHYSICAL!

*I*n this chapter, we delve into the world of movement and exercise—a vital component of your journey toward optimal health. Don't worry if you're feeling a bit out of shape or haven't exercised in a while. The beauty of this journey is that you can start at your own pace, with plenty of modifications available to suit your needs. Regardless of where you begin, rest assured that you'll still reap numerous benefits from even the gentlest modified approach.

Before we begin, let me clarify that throughout this chapter, I'll be using the terms "exercise" and "movement" interchangeably. The key takeaway is that we're talking about getting your body in motion, no matter what you choose to call it.

If the thought of starting an exercise program feels daunting, I completely understand. I, too, once led a sedentary lifestyle while grappling with undiagnosed health issues. It wasn't until I reached the age of 55 that I finally decided to get moving. And guess what? Now, as I pen these words, I'm a vibrant 59-year-old, currently training for my first bikini competition. If I can do it, so can you!

However, it's crucial to emphasize here the importance of consulting with your licensed health-care practitioner before you begin any exercise regimen. Your safety and well-being are paramount, and your health-care provider can help ensure that the exercises you choose are suitable for your individual circumstances.

Always listen to your body and honor its unique needs. If any movement causes discomfort, pain, or simply doesn't feel right, don't hesitate to discontinue it. Reach out to your health coach, trainer, or health-care provider for guidance before resuming any activity.

Let's get into the general benefits of exercise:

1. **Physical health:** Regular exercise helps maintain a healthy weight, lowers the risk of chronic conditions like heart disease, type 2 diabetes, and certain types of cancer. It also enhances cardiovascular fitness, strengthens bones, and improves overall physical functioning.

2. **Menopause management:** Exercise can alleviate common symptoms of menopause, such as hot flashes, mood swings, and sleep disturbances. It may also reduce the risk of osteoporosis, which becomes more prevalent during this stage.

3. **Mental well-being:** Physical activity is linked to improved mental health and a reduced risk of depression and anxiety. It promotes the release of endorphins, neurotransmitters that boost mood and reduce stress.

4. **Cognitive function:** Exercise has been associated with better cognitive function, memory, and concentration. Regular

physical activity may help reduce the risk of age-related cognitive decline, including dementia and Alzheimer's disease.

5. **Strength and flexibility:** Maintaining strength and flexibility is crucial for overall functionality and independence. Exercise, including resistance training and flexibility exercises, helps preserve muscle mass, joint mobility, and balance, reducing the risk of falls and fractures.

6. **Energy and vitality:** Regular exercise enhances energy levels and combats fatigue. It improves stamina and endurance, allowing midlife women to engage in daily activities with ease and maintain an active lifestyle.

7. **Social connections:** Participating in group exercises or fitness classes can provide opportunities for social interaction, fostering a sense of community and support among midlife women. This social engagement contributes to overall well-being.

8. **Weight management:** As metabolism slows down with age, it becomes more challenging to maintain a healthy weight. Exercise helps burn calories, build lean muscle mass, and boost metabolism, aiding in weight management and preventing weight gain.

9. **Disease prevention:** Engaging in regular physical activity lowers the risk of various diseases, including certain cancers, cardiovascular disease, stroke, and metabolic disorders like diabetes. It also improves the body's immune system, reducing susceptibility to infections.

10. **Quality of life:** Exercise plays a crucial role in enhancing overall quality of life for women in midlife and beyond. It promotes a positive body image, self-confidence, and a

sense of accomplishment. It can also improve sleep quality and contribute to a greater sense of well-being.

As you can see, there are many benefits to be derived from exercise.

Now on to strength training and resistance training. This type of exercise is very beneficial for everyone, but especially for women in midlife and beyond. Maintaining muscle is very important, as we saw in the chapter on protein.

What's the difference between resistance training and strength training?

Strength training and resistance training are often used interchangeably because they share similarities and are closely related. However, they are not exactly the same thing.

According to EVO Fitness (https://evofitness.at/en/resistance-training/):

"Resistance-training exercises involve pushing or pulling against the resistance of an object (including your own body), whereas strength training involves a large amount of muscle tissue by continuously increasing the weight you lift (while lowering the number of reps), which leads to bigger body gains in strength."

Strength training is a specific type of resistance training that focuses on increasing strength and power. While all strength training falls under the umbrella of resistance training, not all resistance training exercises are necessarily focused on strength gains.

I use the two terms interchangeably, but I wanted to mention the difference here.

I want to emphasize the importance of strength and resistance training for women in midlife and beyond. Here are some benefits:

1. **Increased muscle strength:** As women age, they tend to experience muscle loss and decreased strength. Strength training helps counteract this by building and maintaining muscle mass, enhancing overall strength, and improving functional abilities. This is crucial for maintaining independence and carrying out daily activities with ease.

2. **Enhanced bone health:** Aging women are more susceptible to osteoporosis and bone fractures. Resistance training stimulates bone remodeling, leading to increased bone density and reduced risk of fractures. It can be particularly beneficial for postmenopausal women who are at a higher risk of bone loss.

3. **Improved joint function and flexibility:** Regular strength-training exercises can enhance joint stability, mobility, and flexibility. Strengthening the muscles around the joints provides better support, reduces the risk of injury, and improves overall joint function, making daily movements more comfortable and efficient.

4. **Increased metabolism and weight management:** Strength training can help increase muscle mass, which in turn boosts the metabolism. As women age, their metabolism tends to slow down, leading to weight gain. Engaging in regular resistance training can counteract this effect by increasing calorie expenditure and supporting healthy weight management.

5. **Improved body composition:** Strength training can lead to positive changes in body composition, such as a decrease in body fat and an increase in lean muscle mass. This can result in a more toned appearance and improved body shape, enhancing self-esteem and body confidence.

6. **Enhanced cardiovascular health:** While strength training is not focused primarily on cardiovascular fitness, it can still have positive effects on heart health. Some studies suggest that resistance training can improve cardiovascular function, reduce blood pressure, and improve lipid profiles in older women.

7. **Mental health benefits:** Engaging in regular strength training can have positive effects on mental well-being. It can reduce symptoms of depression and anxiety, enhance mood and self-esteem, and contribute to a more positive body image.

8. **Reduced risk of chronic diseases:** Strength training has been associated with a reduced risk of chronic conditions, including type 2 diabetes and cardiovascular disease. Regular exercise helps regulate blood-sugar levels, improve insulin sensitivity, and reduce inflammation, leading to a lower risk of developing these conditions.

To sum it up, strength training is very important—especially with aging!

So where to begin with exercise?

Let's start with walking. Walking is not to be underrated! It is my favorite movement. According to www.prevention.com, benefits of walking include:

- Improves your mood
- Burns calories and helps to maintain a healthy weight
- Reduces your risk of chronic disease
- Helps you live longer

- Boosts your brainpower
- Alleviates joint pain
- Delays the onset of varicose veins
- Stimulates your digestive system
- Enhances creativity
- Improves your sleep
- Kickstarts your immune system

A daily walk is an excellent supplement to your life, especially if you live in an area where you have walking trails, a park, a neighborhood, or an open nature area. Whenever possible, walking outdoors in nature is ideal. Being in nature balances cortisol levels (the stress hormone), which in turn helps with attaining your health goals. But even if you cannot walk outdoors due to climate conditions, walking on an indoor treadmill is beneficial.

How long should you walk? The goal is 20 minutes a day, but even shorter periods will still be beneficial. Walk 10 minutes a day as a minimum, with 20 minutes being the ideal.

For walking and indeed any movement regimen, small actions done consistently are very effective. My clients get great results with this approach. However, if you walk for 30 to 60 minutes three times a week because you work 12-hour shifts that turn into 15-hour shifts, you will still get benefits. But if you can break things down into smaller steps done more often and more consistently, it becomes a habit, a part of your everyday life, which is a huge win.

Another great form of movement is yoga.

According to https://www.yogajournal.com/, yoga:

- Improves your flexibility
- Builds muscle strength
- Perfects your posture
- Prevents cartilage and joint breakdown
- Protects your spine
- Improves your bone health
- Drains your lymph and boosts immunity
- Makes you happier
- Helps you focus
- Gives you peace of mind
- Helps you sleep more deeply
- Eases pain

Major universities are on board with the benefits of yoga, as well. According to Harvard Health Publishing, the benefits of yoga include:

- A better body image
- Becoming a mindful eater
- A boost to weight loss and maintenance
- Enhancing fitness
- Cardiovascular benefits

There are different types of yoga. A popular type is hatha yoga, which typically involves a set of physical postures and breathing techniques, practiced more slowly and with more static posture holds than a faster-paced type of yoga such as Vinyasa flow.

My recommendation is to do some form of yoga (or stretching) daily or on most days. Even if it is for only a very short period of time, you'll enjoy the benefits from it. (If you do a session as short as 10 minutes or two to three poses, your mind and body will thank you.)

You can find countless free yoga videos on YouTube. If you type in "yoga 10-minute YouTube" in a Google search, many options will appear. If you're new to yoga, add in the words "beginner" or "gentle" to match your level.

Before getting into more exercises, other than yoga and walking, generally allow at least one rest day in between exercise days, or if you do upper body one day, you can do lower body the next day, but still do allow your body to rest with full rest days off. The 28-Day Kickstart Plan will include exercises for three days a week with at least one rest day in between each day.

Next up are squats.

Squats are a great functional exercise, highly effective for strengthening and toning the lower body. A lot of ground is covered with this one movement—the quadriceps, hamstrings, and glutes. It is a powerful exercise!

Here are step-by-step instructions on how to perform a basic squat:

Basic squat:

1. Stand with your feet slightly wider than hip-width apart, toes pointing slightly outward.

2. Engage your core muscles by drawing your navel toward your spine and keeping your chest lifted.

3. Begin the movement by bending your knees and hips, as if you're sitting back into a chair. Keep your weight in your heels.

4. Lower your body until your thighs are parallel to the floor, or as close as you can comfortably go. Avoid letting your knees extend beyond your toes.

5. Pause for a moment at the bottom of the squat, then exhale and push through your heels to return to the starting position.

If you're just starting out with squats or have concerns about your mobility or stability, start with chair squats. These are gentler on the joints and can help you build strength gradually.

Chair squat:

1. Start by standing in front of a sturdy chair or bench with your feet hip-width apart.

2. Engage your core muscles by drawing your navel toward your spine and keeping your chest lifted.

3. Extend your arms forward for balance or place your hands on your hips.

4. Begin the movement by bending your knees and hips, as if you're going to sit back onto the chair.

5. Lower your body until your glutes lightly touch the chair, while keeping your weight in your heels.

6. Pause for a moment, then engage your leg muscles and push through your heels to stand back up.

How often should these be done?

Some online resources suggest no more than two to three times a week and others specify that squats can be done daily (based on the premise that we're doing squats daily when going from sitting to standing positions throughout the day). It really depends on the intensity and your fitness level.

As a general initial goal, doing 45 squats 3 times a week is recommended.

Break up the squats into 3 sets of 15, with 60 seconds of rest between sets. If that is too intense for your current fitness level, decrease the sets and reduce the reps as needed. Also, increase your rest time in between sets as needed. If needed, you can start with a total of 5–10 squats 3 times a week, depending on your current fitness level. Always honor your body and you can build from there.

Next are planks. Like squats, planks are a great functional exercise.

Performing planks:

- Improves core definition
- Boosts metabolism (great calorie burn!)
- Improves posture
- Improves balance
- Improves flexibility (extends muscle groups)
- May lower risk of back injury

A word of caution regarding planks: If you've had prolapse, prolapse surgery, pelvic conditions, recent childbirth, obesity, or chronic low-back pain, consult your licensed health-care practitioner before starting planks.

As with squats, you can do modified versions of the exercise that will still be beneficial.

Here are step-by-step instructions on how to do a plank:

1. Begin by positioning yourself face down on the floor or exercise mat.

2. Place your hands directly beneath your shoulders, fingers spread wide for stability.

3. Extend your legs straight behind you, with your toes pressed firmly to the ground.

4. Engage your core muscles by drawing your navel toward your spine.

5. Ensure that your body forms a straight line from head to toe, with your neck and spine in a neutral position.

6. Maintain a strong, stable position by squeezing your glutes and thigh muscles.

7. Keep your gaze focused downward to maintain a neutral neck position.

8. Hold the full plank position for the desired amount of time.

9. Breathe steadily throughout the exercise, avoiding holding your breath.

10. When you're ready to finish, slowly lower your knees to the floor and release the position.

Remember to maintain proper form throughout the exercise. Avoid sagging or lifting your hips too high. If you find it difficult to hold the full plank initially, you can modify it by performing the exercise on your forearms instead of your hands. With consistent practice, you can gradually increase your strength and endurance.

If full planks are too intense, knee planks may be a good option for you. Here are step-by-step instructions.

Knee planks:

1. Start by positioning yourself on all fours, with your hands directly beneath your shoulders and knees beneath your hips.

2. Lower your knees to the ground, ensuring they are positioned hip-width apart.

3. Place your hands firmly on the ground, fingers spread wide for stability.

4. Engage your core muscles by drawing your navel toward your spine.

5. Extend your legs straight behind you, but keep your toes lifted off the ground. Your weight should be supported by your knees.

6. Ensure that your body forms a straight line from your head to your knees, with your neck and spine in a neutral position.

7. Maintain a strong, stable position by squeezing your glutes and thigh muscles.

8. Keep your gaze focused downward to maintain a neutral neck position.

9. Hold the knee plank position for the desired amount of time.

10. Breathe steadily throughout the exercise, avoiding holding your breath.

11. When you're ready to finish, slowly lift your knees off the ground and return to the starting position on all fours.

If doing planks on the ground is too intense and the knee planks are hard on your knees, you can try wall planks, as follows:

Wall planks:

1. Find a clear wall space with enough room for you to lean against comfortably.

2. Stand facing the wall, about a foot or two away from it.

3. Place your hands flat on the wall at shoulder height, slightly wider than shoulder-width apart.

4. Lean your body forward and walk your feet backward, maintaining a straight line from your head to your heels.

5. As you walk your feet back, allow your body to tilt forward until your arms are fully extended and your body is at an angle.

6. Press your palms firmly to the wall and engage your core muscles by drawing your navel toward your spine.

7. Ensure that your body forms a straight line from your head to your heels, with your neck and spine in a neutral position.

8. Keep your gaze forward and avoid sagging or arching your back.

9. Hold the wall plank position for the desired amount of time.

10. Breathe steadily throughout the exercise, avoiding holding your breath.

11. When you're ready to finish, slowly walk your feet back toward the wall and return to a standing position.

How long should a plank be held?

It depends on your fitness level. Start with holding for 10 seconds and incrementally work up to 30 seconds as a higher-end goal. If you do not achieve 30 seconds, you still get benefits from planks. Note that you can go longer than 30 seconds if you are at a higher level of fitness. But 30 seconds is a really good goal.

How often should planks be done?

Like squats, there are differing opinions on this. Proponents for doing them daily indicate this is safe because you're not breaking down a lot of muscle fibers.

As a general initial goal, I recommend doing planks 3 times a week and do 3 sets of planks at each session with a 30-second rest between sets (take longer rest periods if needed). You can start with holding the plank for 5–10 seconds and incrementally increase to 30 seconds (or beyond if your fitness level is high).

It's best to do squats and planks after your body has been warmed up, such as after your daily walk. However, these are more "functional" or natural movements for the body, so an argument can be made that warming up isn't mandatory. Generally speaking, though, warming up before these kinds of exercises is always helpful in my opinion and reduces the risk of injury (regardless of your fitness level).

If it's not convenient to do squats and planks after your walk, you can do "knee ups," "butt kickers," or march in place for 3 minutes to warm up your body. You can do 3 sets of 1 minute each, with a 30-second rest in between, and if that's too much, you can break it down to 6 sets of 30 seconds each with a 30-second rest. Take longer rest periods if needed.

After completing the squats and planks exercises, it would be ideal to do your 10 minutes of yoga, if this can be managed and your schedule allows.

Additional exercises to build onto squats and planks:

These next exercises can all be done at home and no gym equipment is required (except for one exercise that calls for dumbbells—arm raises; however, a very low weight is strongly recommended for these, and soup cans or single-serving water bottles will suffice).

These can be done 3 times a week on the same days as you do your squats and planks. And as mentioned with squats and planks, it's best to do exercises after your body has been warmed up, such as after your walk, or you can do "knee ups," "butt kickers," or march in place.

There are so many wonderful exercises available, but here are some to give you a good start. (A wide range of reps is given to allow you to adjust to your individual fitness level accordingly.)

Double leg-drop: 3 sets, 5–10 reps each set:

1. Lie on your back on a mat or a flat surface. Extend your legs fully and place your arms by your sides, palms facing down.

2. Engage your core muscles by pulling your navel toward your spine. This will help stabilize your lower back throughout the exercise.

3. Keeping your legs together, lift them off the ground toward the ceiling. Your feet should be directly above your hips, and your legs should be perpendicular to the floor. This is your starting position.

4. In a controlled manner, slowly lower both legs toward the floor without touching the ground. Keep your lower back pressed against the mat or floor throughout the movement.

5. Continue lowering your legs until you feel your lower back start to lift off the mat. At this point, pause and hold for a second.

6. Slowly raise your legs back to the starting position by engaging your lower abs. Focus on using your core muscles rather than momentum to lift your legs.

7. Repeat the movement for the desired number of repetitions. Start with a lower number of repetitions, such as 8–10, and gradually increase as you become more comfortable and stronger.

Tips for performing the double leg-drop exercise:

- Make sure to maintain a controlled movement throughout the exercise and avoid any jerking or swinging motions.
- Keep your breathing steady and exhale as you lower your legs, and inhale as you raise them back up.
- If you find it challenging to keep your lower back pressed against the mat, you can modify the exercise by bending your knees slightly or placing your hands underneath your hips for added support.
- It's important to listen to your body and work within your comfort level. If you experience any pain or discomfort, stop the exercise and consult with a fitness professional.

Bicycle crunch: 3 sets, 8-15 each side for each set

1. Lie flat on your back on an exercise mat or the floor. Place your hands lightly behind your head, keeping your elbows open and your fingers touching your temples. Alternatively, you can cross your arms over your chest.

2. Lift your legs off the ground, bending your knees at a 90-degree angle. Your thighs should be perpendicular to the floor and your calves parallel to the floor. This is your starting position.

3. Engage your core by drawing your navel toward your spine. This will help stabilize your lower back throughout the exercise.

4. Start the movement by simultaneously bringing your right knee toward your chest while lifting your upper body off the ground. As you do this, twist your torso to the right, bringing your left elbow toward your right knee.

5. At the same time, extend your left leg straight out, keeping it a few inches off the floor. Your left foot should be flexed.

6. Pause briefly at the top of the movement, making sure to exhale as you contract your abs.

7. Return to the starting position by reversing the movement. Straighten your right leg while simultaneously bringing your left knee toward your chest. Twist your torso to the left, bringing your right elbow toward your left knee.

8. Continue alternating sides in a pedaling motion, as if you were riding a bicycle. Focus on keeping your core engaged and your movements controlled throughout the exercise.

9. Aim for a smooth and rhythmic motion, maintaining a steady pace throughout your set. It's important to avoid pulling on your head or neck with your hands; instead, use your abs to lift your upper body.

10. Repeat the exercise for the desired number of repetitions or time duration.

Glute bridge: 3 sets, 8–12 reps each set

1. Lie flat on your back on an exercise mat or the floor with your knees bent and feet flat on the ground. Your feet should be hip-width apart, and your arms should be relaxed by your sides.

2. Engage your core muscles by gently drawing your navel toward your spine. This will help stabilize your spine throughout the exercise.

3. Press your feet into the ground, ensuring that your heels are firmly planted. This will be your starting position.

4. Begin the movement by pushing through your heels and lifting your hips off the ground. As you lift your hips, squeeze your glutes (the muscles in your buttocks) and keep your core engaged.

5. Continue lifting until your hips and knees form a straight line. Your shoulders, hips, and knees should be in alignment. Avoid overextending your lower back or arching your spine excessively.

6. Pause at the top of the movement for a second, focusing on squeezing your glutes.

7. Slowly lower your hips back down to the starting position, keeping control of the movement and engaging your glutes throughout.

Kneeling push-ups: 3 sets, 3–8 each set

1. Start by positioning yourself on the floor or an exercise mat. Get down on your hands and knees, with your hands slightly wider than shoulder-width apart.

2. Extend your legs behind you and cross your ankles, so your weight is supported on your hands and knees (you don't have to cross your ankles, but it may provide more stability).

3. Keep your back straight and engage your core muscles to maintain a stable body position.

4. Lower your chest toward the floor by bending your elbows. Lower yourself until your chest is just above the ground or as far as you can comfortably go.

5. Pause briefly at the bottom position and then push yourself back up by straightening your arms, while keeping your body in a straight line.

Tips for proper form:

- Keep your head in a neutral position, looking slightly ahead, to maintain a straight line from your head to your hips.

- Engage your core muscles throughout the exercise to stabilize your body and prevent your lower back from sagging.

- Focus on controlling the movement and maintaining a slow and controlled tempo.

- Breathe steadily throughout the exercise, inhaling as you lower your chest and exhaling as you push back up.

Wall push-ups (if the knee push-ups are too intense): 3 sets, 3–8 each set

1. Stand facing a wall, approximately arm's length away. Make sure you have enough space to extend your arms fully.

2. Position your feet shoulder-width apart. Your toes should be pointing forward.

3. Place your palms flat against the wall at shoulder height and slightly wider than shoulder-width apart. Your fingers should be pointing upward or slightly inward.

4. Engage your core muscles by tightening your abdominal muscles and maintaining a neutral spine position.

5. Lean your body forward and bend your elbows, allowing your chest to approach the wall. Keep your head aligned with your spine, looking straight ahead.

6. Continue leaning forward until your nose or chest gently touches the wall. Your elbows should be at a 90-degree angle at the bottom position.

7. Push through your palms and extend your arms to return to the starting position. Keep your body straight and avoid arching or sagging your lower back.

Additional tips:

- Breathe in as you lower your body toward the wall and exhale as you push back up.

- Focus on maintaining a controlled movement throughout the exercise.

- Keep your body aligned and avoid excessive leaning or swinging.

- If you experience any discomfort or pain, stop the exercise and consult a health-care professional.

Standing arm raises (front and lateral): Standing arm front raises: 3 sets, 6–12 reps each set

1. Start with a low weight, even 1 to 2 pounds. It takes only a little bit of weight for this workout to be effective and it's a more intense exercise as it is.

2. Stand with your feet shoulder-width apart, keeping your back straight and core engaged.

3. Hold a dumbbell in each hand with an overhand grip (palms facing your thighs) and let your arms hang straight down in front of your body.

4. Slowly lift one arm straight out in front of you while keeping it slightly bent at the elbow. Continue lifting until your arm is parallel to the floor, at shoulder height or just below your shoulders.

5. Pause briefly at the top of the movement.

6. Slowly lower the dumbbell back down to the starting position, controlling the movement.

7. Repeat the movement with the opposite arm.

Standing arm lateral raises: 3 sets, 6–12 reps each set

1. Like the front raises, start with a low weight (even as low as 1 to 2 pounds). It takes only a little bit of weight for this workout to be effective and it's a more intense exercise as it is. (The weight you use for the lateral raises may be less than what you use for the front raises—I find this is often the case for my clients and for me.)

2. Stand with your feet shoulder-width apart, maintaining good posture with your back straight and core engaged.

3. Hold a dumbbell in each hand with an overhand grip (palms facing your thighs) and let your arms hang straight down at your sides.

4. Keeping a slight bend in your elbows, simultaneously raise both arms out to the sides until they are parallel to the floor, or slightly below shoulder level (don't go higher than shoulder level).

5. Lateral raises should be around 20 degrees in front of your chest, not in a straight line, in order to protect the rotator cuff.

6. Pause briefly at the top of the movement.

7. Slowly lower the dumbbells back down to the starting position, controlling the movement.

Important tips for both exercises:

- Maintain a controlled and smooth movement throughout, avoiding any swinging or jerking motions.

- Focus on using the targeted muscles (shoulders) to lift the dumbbells rather than relying on momentum.

- Start with lighter weights and gradually increase the resistance as you become more comfortable and stronger.

- If you feel any discomfort or pain, reduce the weight or stop the exercise and consult with a fitness professional.

- Breathe naturally throughout the exercises, exhaling during the lifting phase and inhaling during the lowering phase.

Lunges (forward and reverse): Forward lunge: 3 sets, 6–12 each side for each set

1. Stand tall with your feet hip-width apart and your arms relaxed at your sides.

2. Take a step forward with your right foot, landing on the heel first and rolling onto the ball of your foot.

3. Lower your body down by bending both knees, ensuring that your right knee is directly above your ankle and your left knee is hovering above the ground.

4. Keep your torso upright and your core engaged. Your back should be straight, and your chest lifted.

5. Pause briefly in the lunge position, then push through your right heel to straighten your right leg and return to the starting position.

6. Repeat the movement by stepping forward with your left foot, alternating legs for the desired number of repetitions.

Reverse lunge: 3 sets, 6–12 each side for each set

1. Stand tall with your feet hip-width apart and your arms relaxed at your sides.

2. Take a step backward with your right foot, landing on the ball of your foot first and then lowering your heel to the ground.

3. Lower your body down by bending both knees, making sure your left knee is directly above your ankle and your right knee is hovering above the ground.

4. Keep your torso upright, engage your core, and maintain a straight back and lifted chest.

5. Pause briefly in the lunge position, then push through your left heel to straighten your left leg and return to the starting position.

6. Repeat the movement by stepping backward with your left foot, alternating legs for the desired number of repetitions.

Tips:

- Keep your movements controlled and avoid rushing through the exercise.

- Maintain proper form by keeping your knees aligned with your toes and not letting them extend beyond your toes.
- Engage your core muscles to help stabilize your body throughout the movement.
- To increase the difficulty, you can hold dumbbells or a barbell on your shoulders.
- Start with a comfortable range of motion and gradually increase the depth of your lunges as you become more comfortable and flexible.

If any exercise is too intense for your current fitness level, you can:

- Increase the sets and reduce the reps, and/or
- increase your rest time in between sets.
- Or if the exercise is still too difficult, start with doing 1 set total and decrease the reps by half (or less if needed).

After completing your exercise routine, you can do either 10 minutes of yoga as a post-exercise stretch routine or some basic post-exercise stretches, as follows.

Knee to chest: Hold 15–30 seconds each for each side. One set.

1. Start by lying on your back on a comfortable surface, such as a yoga mat or a carpeted floor.
2. Bend both knees and keep your feet flat on the ground.
3. Place your hands on your thighs, just above your knees.
4. Take a deep breath.
5. As you exhale, slowly bring one knee toward your chest by gently pulling it with your hands. You can interlace your fingers behind your thigh to assist in the movement.

6. Hold this position for 15 to 30 seconds, feeling a gentle stretch in your lower back and glutes. It's important not to force the movement or go beyond your comfort level.

7. Keep your other leg relaxed, with your foot still on the ground.

8. After the desired duration, slowly release the stretched leg and return it to the starting position.

9. Repeat the same steps with the opposite leg.

Tips:

- Focus on keeping your head, shoulders, and neck relaxed throughout the stretch.

- Maintain a slow and controlled breathing pattern. Inhale deeply before starting the stretch and exhale slowly as you bring your knee toward your chest.

- If you have any lower back or hip pain, it's advisable to consult with a health-care professional before attempting this exercise.

Quad Stretch, standing or lying: If standing, hold onto something for support/balance. Do 1 set each side, hold 15–30 seconds each time.

Standing quad stretch

1. Stand upright with your feet hip-width apart.

2. Find a stable support, such as a wall or a chair, to maintain your balance.

3. Shift your weight onto one leg.

4. Bend your other knee and bring your heel toward your buttocks.

5. Reach back with the same-side hand and grab your ankle or foot.

6. Gently pull your foot toward your buttocks until you feel a stretch in the front of your thigh (quadriceps).

7. Keep your knees close together and your torso upright.

8. Hold the stretch for 15 to 30 seconds, while maintaining a relaxed breathing pattern.

9. Slowly release the stretch and repeat on the other side.

Lying quad stretch:

1. Lie face down on a comfortable surface, such as a yoga mat or a padded exercise mat.

2. Extend your legs fully behind you.

3. Prop yourself up onto your forearms, keeping your elbows directly under your shoulders.

4. Alternatively, you can do this lying on your side instead, with your arm that is closer to the ground overhead with your head/neck resting on that arm.

5. Bend one knee and bring your heel toward your buttocks. (If you're lying on your side, it's the knee on the ceiling side, not the knee you're lying on.)

6. Reach back with the same-side hand and grab your ankle or foot.

7. Gently pull your foot toward your buttocks until you feel a stretch in the front of your thigh.

8. Keep your knees close together and avoid arching your lower back excessively.

9. Hold the stretch for 15 to 30 seconds, maintaining a relaxed breathing pattern.

10. Slowly release the stretch and repeat on the other side.

Tips:

- While performing both standing and lying quad stretches, remember to keep your body stable and avoid any excessive bouncing or jerking movements.

- If balance is a concern during the standing quad stretch, you can perform it near a wall or use a chair for support.

- It's important to listen to your body and stretch within your comfort range. If you feel any pain or discomfort, ease off the stretch or stop if necessary.

- Remember to breathe deeply and relax your muscles throughout the stretching process.

Supine figure-four hip stretch: Do 1 set each side, hold 15–30 seconds each time.

1. Lie on your back with both knees bent and feet flat on the ground.

2. Cross your right ankle over your left thigh, forming a "figure 4" shape.

3. Reach through the space between your legs and interlace your hands behind your left thigh.

4. Gently pull your left thigh toward your chest until you feel a stretch in your right hip and glute.

5. Hold the stretch for 15 to 30 seconds and then switch sides.

6. Remember to relax and breathe deeply during each stretch.

Shoulder rolls, 2 sets each way: Roll backward for 5 rolls, then roll forward for 5 rolls and repeat for a second set.

1. Stand with your feet shoulder-width apart and your arms relaxed at your sides.

2. Roll your shoulders backward in a circular motion, starting with small circles and gradually increasing the size of the circles.

3. Perform 5 backward shoulder rolls, focusing on maintaining a smooth and controlled movement.

4. After completing the backward rolls, switch to forward rolls. Roll your shoulders forward in a circular motion, again starting with small circles and gradually increasing them.

5. Perform 5 forward shoulder rolls, ensuring that the movement is smooth and controlled.

6. As you roll your shoulders, try to relax your neck and upper back, allowing the movement to be fluid and natural.

7. If you experience any pain or discomfort during the shoulder rolls, reduce the range of motion or stop the exercise.

Shoulder cross stretch, 1 set each side: Hold for 15–30 seconds each side.

1. Stand or sit up straight.

2. Extend your right arm straight in front of you at shoulder level.

3. Take your left arm and cross it over your chest, reaching for your right arm.

4. Use your left arm to gently pull your right arm closer to your chest, feeling a stretch in the back of your right shoulder.

5. Hold the stretch for about 15–30 seconds.

6. Repeat on the other side, crossing your left arm over your chest and using your right arm to pull it closer.

7. Remember to breathe deeply and avoid any movements that cause pain or discomfort.

Please note: With *any* movements or exercises, do not overdo it! Honor your body's abilities and condition. With any movement or exercise regime, be careful and get your licensed health-care practitioner's approval before starting an exercise plan.

Hey, what about cardio?

No, I haven't forgotten cardio exercise. However, too much of it can work against your health goals, especially weight-loss goals. This is because it causes a significant stress response in the body (increased cortisol) and this extra stress works against you by keeping fat tissue on the body. When the body is stressed, it "hangs onto" fat tissue as a safety mechanism, which isn't helpful.

Cardio exercises such as the elliptical, treadmill, and rower are great, but women in midlife and beyond need to have a bigger focus on strength and resistance training. Yes, you can still incorporate cardio into your exercise plan, but not daily (walking daily, yes; cardio daily, no).

For the 28-Day Kickstart Plan, the only recommended exercise related to cardio is walking. But after the 28-day kickstart, I do recommend incorporating cardio into your regimen—just don't overdo it!

When you do add cardio to your regimen, High Intensity Interval Training (HIIT) is recommended.

Here are some key advantages of HIIT:

1. **Time-efficient:** HIIT workouts typically involve short bursts of intense exercise followed by brief recovery periods. This approach allows you to achieve maximum benefits in a shorter amount of time than with traditional steady-state cardio workouts. This is particularly advantageous for busy midlife women who may have limited time for exercise.

2. **Increased calorie burn:** HIIT workouts can help boost your metabolism and calorie burn during and after the exercise session. The intense bursts of activity require more energy, leading to a higher calorie expenditure. This can be beneficial for weight management and maintaining a healthy body composition.

3. **Improved cardiovascular fitness:** HIIT exercises are known for their ability to elevate heart rate and challenge the cardiovascular system. Regular participation in HIIT workouts can enhance cardiovascular endurance, leading to a stronger heart and improved overall cardiovascular health. This is especially important for midlife women, as the risk of heart disease tends to increase with age.

4. **Muscle preservation and strength:** As women age, they naturally experience a decline in muscle mass. However, HIIT workouts that incorporate resistance-training elements can help preserve and build lean muscle. Increased

muscle mass not only contributes to a toned appearance but also improves metabolic rate, bone health, and overall strength.

5. **Enhanced insulin sensitivity:** HIIT has been shown to improve insulin sensitivity, which is the body's ability to utilize insulin effectively for blood-sugar regulation. As we saw in "Chapter 10," midlife women are at an increased risk of developing insulin resistance, so improving insulin sensitivity through HIIT can help mitigate these risks.

6. **Hormonal benefits:** Research suggests that HIIT may positively affect hormonal profiles by increasing the production of growth hormone and promoting the release of endorphins, which can improve mood and alleviate some symptoms associated with menopause.

7. **Mental well-being:** HIIT workouts can have a positive effect on mental health by reducing stress levels and improving cognitive function. The intensity of the exercise releases endorphins, which are known as "feel-good" hormones. Additionally, HIIT workouts often incorporate varied and engaging movements, making the exercise sessions more enjoyable and motivating.

Again, it's important to have your licensed health-care practitioner's approval before starting a new exercise program.

If you're new to HIIT workouts, start with one HIIT session per week and build up to two to three sessions a week. How long you do each session depends on your current fitness level.

Here's how to implement HIIT workouts:

1. **Warm up.** Begin each HIIT session with a warm-up to prepare your body for exercise (just as with your strength-training plan).

2. **Start with shorter intervals.** Begin with shorter work and rest intervals to allow your body to adapt gradually. For example, start with 20 seconds of intense exercise followed by 40 seconds of rest or active recovery. As you become more comfortable, you can gradually increase the intensity and duration of the intervals. If you're new to HIIT training, start with three sessions of the 20-second intense exercise followed by 40 seconds of rest cycle (and if that's too intense, reduce it to one or two cycles).

3. **Choose low-impact exercises.** Select exercises that are low-impact to reduce stress on the joints and minimize the risk of injury. Examples include marching in place, step-ups, modified jumping jacks, stationary biking, or using an elliptical machine.

4. **Modify exercises if necessary.** If any exercises feel too challenging or uncomfortable, you can modify them to suit your fitness level and capabilities. Listen to your body. Pay attention to your body's signals and adjust the intensity or duration as needed. It's essential to push yourself, but not to the point of pain or excessive strain.

5. **Gradually increase intensity and duration.** As you progress and feel more comfortable, gradually increase the intensity and duration of your HIIT workouts. You can lengthen the work intervals, reduce the rest intervals, or incorporate more challenging exercises.

6. **Include proper rest and recovery.** Allow your body enough time to rest and recover between HIIT sessions. This is crucial for preventing overexertion and reducing the risk of injury.

7. Remember to **stay hydrated** before, during, and after your workouts.

Remember the benefits of exercise, and embrace it as a powerful tool for enhancing your overall well-being!

PART FOUR

Let's Go!

CHAPTER 14

✦

HELPFUL FOOD-PREP TIPS FOR THE 28-DAY KICKSTART PLAN

Welcome to the world of delicious and healthy meal prep! If you're looking for a way to streamline your cooking process, save time, and still enjoy nutritious meals throughout the week, you're in the right place. Let's dive into some meal-prep tips that will revolutionize the way you approach your kitchen adventures.

Meal prep is like having a personal assistant in the kitchen, helping you stay on track with your health goals while making your life a whole lot easier. By dedicating some time upfront to plan and prepare your meals, you'll reap the benefits of stress-free eating during busy weekdays.

Meal prep does require a bit of time and effort in the beginning, but as you get the hang of it and make it a regular practice, you'll become a meal-prep pro, efficiently whipping up tasty dishes like a seasoned chef. Instead of scrambling to figure out what to cook each night or resorting to unhealthy takeout, you'll open your fridge to a lineup of thoughtfully prepared meals, ready to be enjoyed at your convenience.

The beauty of meal prep lies in its flexibility. There are countless recipe variations you can explore, catering to your unique tastes and dietary preferences. If you're seeking inspiration, check out the many online resources and YouTube videos available on this topic.

Whether you're a seasoned meal prepper or just starting, the following tips will set you on the right path. Let's get your meal-prep routine rolling so you can savor the benefits of nourishing, time-saving meals.

Here are some ideas to get you started.

Tacos

- Homemade taco meat with ground turkey or ground beef is a great meal prep go-to. This stores well in the freezer, too.
  - Avoid the store-bought packets of taco seasoning. It's best to make your own; however, if you do purchase seasoning, gluten-free and MSG-free seasonings are recommended. But making your own is easy. There is a taco meat recipe coming up in "Appendix A."
  - Serve the prepped taco meat on mixed greens/lettuce or cauliflower rice, or make a burrito bowl (with avocado and salsa along with a squeeze of lime).

Marinated Chicken Breasts

- This is one of my favorite meal prep go-tos! Marinate several chicken breasts in a good marinade for 30 minutes to

6 hours (without industrial vegetable and seed oils such as soybean, canola, or safflower).

○ Use Primal Kitchen brand marinade (Greek, Italian, Cilantro Lime, Balsamic Vinaigrette) or prepare a basic homemade marinade with avocado oil, lemon juice, or red wine vinegar, and seasonings of your choice.

○ Cook the chicken breasts (bake or grill—I use a large George Foreman grill) to 165°F internal temperature. Either freeze them in Ziploc bags for future meals, or:

■ Place them in individual serving containers along with mixed veggies and microwave when ready to eat.

● For the veggies, you can use frozen veggies (there are a lot of good varieties available with carrots, peppers, broccoli, etc., or cut up your own and place in the containers) or a bed of cauliflower rice (slice up lemon or lime wedges in advance and have them ready to go for the chicken/cauliflower rice meal).

■ Serve on lettuce salads or on a bed of cauliflower rice.

■ Note that reheated cooked chicken may be on the dry side. Squeeze on lemon juice to remedy this (also, lemon juice on the chicken aids digestion and the vitamin C is beneficial).

Shredded Chicken Breasts

● Shredded chicken breast is great to have prepped in advance. You can have this on hand for the week's meal prep and/or freeze it in Ziploc bags for future meals.

- You can serve it on mixed greens/salads, or as burrito bowls on a bed of cauliflower rice along with sliced avocado, salsa, and lime wedges (avocado needs to be sliced fresh with the meal).

- It's easy to make shredded chicken in a slow cooker. Just take a few pounds of chicken breast and place into the slow cooker. Add a cup of chicken broth and seasonings of your choice. Cook on low for 6–8 hours. Remove the chicken and shred with two forks.

Egg Bake

- Egg bakes are a wonderful option—and not just for breakfast! You can place them in individual serving containers and reheat when ready to serve them. These will store for 3 days, so you don't want to make a week's worth unless you freeze the individual servings.

- Egg bake recipes remind me of chili recipes—there are so many different versions. To simplify things, whisk a dozen eggs, add in any chopped vegetables you like (tomatoes, broccoli, bell peppers, mushrooms, sun-dried tomatoes, etc.), add in chopped cooked bacon or cooked breakfast sausage pieces if you like, pour the mixture into a greased 9x13" pan and bake at 350°F for 35–50 minutes, until a knife inserted in the center comes out clean.

Egg Muffins

- Like the egg bakes, egg muffins are a good go-to.
- Prepare a full tin of them and enjoy them for snacks and/or meals for up to 3 days.

- There are many recipes available online or follow the egg bake recipe above but use a greased muffin tin instead of the pan. These will cook much more quickly than the egg bake and will be done in 15–18 minutes in a 350°F oven.

Slow-Cooker Balsamic Roast Beef

- This is an easy and delicious meal prep recipe. You can serve it on a bed of cauliflower rice or with a side of mixed vegetables (there are many frozen mixed vegetable varieties available) placed in individual containers. This freezes well, too.

- This is very easy to make. Place 3–4 pounds of boneless chuck or round roast into the slow cooker. In a separate bowl, combine a cup of beef broth, ¾ cup of balsamic vinegar, a tablespoon of coconut aminos, one tablespoon of honey, and for an optional extra kick, add in a ½–1 teaspoon of cayenne pepper or red pepper flakes. Cook on low for 6–8 hours. Remove the beef when done and break apart with forks. Pour a cup of the liquid from the slow cooker onto the beef.

Miscellaneous Meal-Prep Tips

- **Pick a date.** Put meal prep time into your weekly calendar (once or twice a week). Treat it like a medical appointment or job interview: make it happen!

- **Plan your meals.** Start by deciding which meals you want to prep for the week. Plan your breakfasts, lunches, dinners, and snacks in advance so you have a clear idea of what you need to prepare.

- **Make a shopping list.** Once you have your meal plan, create a shopping list of all the ingredients you'll need. This will help you stay organized and ensure you have everything on hand when you start prepping.

- **Batch cook proteins.** Prepare a large batch of proteins such as chicken breasts, turkey burgers, beef burgers, or fish at the beginning of the week. Cook them with simple seasonings or healthy homemade marinades to add flavor (or use quality store-bought marinades such as Primal Kitchen brand). Portion them out and refrigerate or freeze for use in various meals throughout the week.

- **Pre-cut vegetables.** Wash, chop, and portion out vegetables in advance. This saves time when you're ready to assemble meals and ensures you have plenty of veggies on hand for salads, stir-fries, or roasting.

- **Use Mason jar salads.** Mason jar salads are a convenient way to prep salads in advance. Layer your ingredients in a jar, starting with the dressing at the bottom, followed by heartier ingredients, and then the greens on top. When you're ready to eat, just shake the jar to mix everything together and pour it into a bowl.

- **Prep citrus.** It's convenient to have sliced lemon and lime wedges ready to go.

  ○ Cut 2–3 lemons or limes into wedges all at once and place them in a container so they're in your refrigerator and ready to go.

  ○ If these are not used up for meals during the week, they can be squeezed into your drinking water.

- **Make homemade sauces and dressings in advance.** Store-bought sauces and dressings often contain additives and preservatives that are not healthy. Instead, make your own using quality ingredients such as avocado oil, olive oil, coconut aminos, balsamic vinegar, herbs, and spices. Store them in airtight containers for easy access.

- **Use a slow cooker.** This can be a time-saving tool for meal prep. Throw in your protein, vegetables, and seasonings, and let them cook throughout the day while you focus on other tasks. Or use an Instant Pot to shorten the cooking window time.

- **Stay organized.** Label your prepped meals with dates and contents to keep track of freshness and prevent waste. Keep an inventory of your freezer and pantry items to know what needs replenishing.

- **Double up.** Double your recipes and freeze the additional portions.

- It's best to store your pre-made meals in microwave-safe glass containers when possible.

  o Chemicals can be released when reheating in plastic. That said, it's better to have meal prep in plastic containers than to eat something unhealthy like fast food. Ziploc bags are also very handy for meal prep.

  o Ideally transfer foods that will be reheated in a microwave to a non-plastic microwave-safe dish when reheating—but do put glass containers on your wish list!

Timesaver Tips

While preparing whole foods is best and my first choice, the timesavers listed below can be a great option when you're tired or you have a busy schedule.

You can purchase the following:

- Frozen pre-riced cauliflower
- Frozen pre-diced sweet potatoes
- Mixed greens in the clamshell containers or pre-cut lettuce sold in bags
  - I would recommend choosing mixed organic greens over the non-organic cut up lettuces. However, while the cut up non-organic lettuces are a "last choice," they're still a better choice than unhealthy foods.
- For sauces and salad dressings, you can purchase a quality product such as Primal Kitchen brand.
- Guacamole/mashed avocados are sold in single-serve containers; these can be a timesaver since avocados generally cannot be prepped in advance.
- Mushrooms.
  - Sautéed fresh mushrooms are best, but when you're extra tired or pressed for time, having mushrooms that are sold in a glass jar can suffice (they're a nice addition to foods and still a better option than processed foods).
- Frozen vegetables.
  - There are so many varieties available, and they heat up easily.
- Meals that can be ordered online. These may be pricey, but if very pressed for time, they're a nice option to have. See "Appendix C: Resources" for some recommendations.

Snacks:

- Have portable healthy snacks available. Healthy snacks such as hard-boiled eggs, guacamole or salsa with pre-cut vegetables, beef or turkey sticks, pickles (check the ingredients for sugar), apples with nut butter, nuts, or homemade trail mix can be prepped and packed in small containers or snack-sized bags.

  - An easy trail mix recipe is 3 parts nuts/seeds of your choice, 2 parts unsweetened coconut chips, and 1 part unsweetened dried fruit. If you can't find unsweetened dried fruit at your local grocery store, these products can be ordered online—from Amazon, for example.

Finally, here's a template that simplifies meal planning.

PROTEIN	CARBS	FATS	SEASONINGS
Bacon	Artichoke hearts	Almonds	Allspice
Beef	Asparagus	Avocado	Apple cider vinegar
Chicken	Beets	Bacon fat	Basil
Cod	Bok choy	Black olives	Bay leaf
Collagen protein	Broccoli	Brazil nuts	Black pepper
Eggs	Brussels sprouts	Butter	Cardamom
Flounder	Cabbage	Coconut butter	Celery seed
Haddock	Carrots	Coconut milk (canned)	Chili powder

PROTEIN	CARBS	FATS	SEASONINGS
Halibut	Cauliflower	Coconut oil	Cilantro
Lamb	Celery	Fish oil	Cinnamon
Mackerel	Chard	Ghee	Clove
Pea protein	Collard greens	Macadamia oil	Cumin
Pork	Cucumber	Mayo (w/o industrial oils)	Curry
Ribs	Green beans	MCT oil	Dill
Salmon	Eggplant	Nut butters	Fenugreek
Sardines	Kale	Olive oil	Garlic
Shrimp	Lettuce (various types)	Palm oil	Mustard seed
Snapper	Mushrooms	Pecans	Nutmeg
Tilapia	Onions	Seeds	Onion
Trout	Peppers	Tallow	Oregano
Tuna	Plantains	Walnuts	Paprika
Turkey	Potatoes (white)		Pepper
Veal	Radish		Rosemary
Venison	Rutabaga		Sea salt
	Spinach		Shallot
	Squash		Thyme
	Sweet potato		Turmeric
	Tomatoes		
	Turnips		

PROTEIN	CARBS	FATS	SEASONINGS
	Yellow summer squash		
	Zucchini		
	Blueberries		
	Blackberries		
	Grapefruit		
	Green apple		
	Lemon		
	Lime		
	Passion fruit		
	Raspberries		
	Strawberries		

Include protein, carbs, and fat in all meals. If your protein is very lean, add additional fat to the meal.

Note: Low-sugar fruits are listed here and these are the best options for balancing blood sugar; however, other fruits are fine in moderate quantities (and depending on whether you're close to meeting or have met your goals).

Be sure to check out "Appendix A" for nutrient-dense, blood-sugar balancing, anti-inflammatory, and gut healing recipes.

CHAPTER 15

❧

THE 28-DAY KICKSTART PLAN

*C*ongratulations! You've learned the essential aspects of this plan. Now, it's time to put everything into action and kickstart your journey to better health. It's time to combine the four pillars of the plan: nutrition, movement (exercise), lifestyle, and mindset.

Think of these plan pillars as powerful building blocks. Each is important on its own, but when you combine them, magic happens. Your results will be even more impressive when you embrace all aspects of this plan.

This journey will bring positive changes to your life. So get ready, stay excited, and let's make these next 28 days incredible. You've got this!

Here are your action items for the next 28 days.

Week 1 (Days 1-7)
Nutrition Pillar:

Drink your water!

- Measure your water intake for a couple days to confirm how much you're drinking.

- If you're drinking less than 75 ounces a day, incrementally increase to 75 ounces a day as a first goal.

- When you meet 75 ounces a day, incrementally increase until you meet the goal of 100 ounces a day.

- It's important to increase gradually so the body can adjust.

- If you feel dizzy, get leg cramps, feel "off," or experience disrupted sleep, then reduce your intake to the amount you were drinking (your body hasn't adjusted yet).

Avoid refined sugar!

- Remove any refined sugar from your pantry, refrigerator, and freezer. If you can't do this due to others in your household not following this plan with you, at least move these products to areas that aren't at eye level.

- Add healthy fats and healthy snacks as described in "Chapter 8: Ditch the Diet Fads" and "Chapter 14: Helpful Food-Prep Tips for the 28-Day Kickstart Plan."

- Consider taking L-glutamine if you have a strong sugar addiction, but do get your licensed health-care practitioner's approval before starting it.

Movement Pillar:
Walk daily!

- Walk a minimum of 10 minutes a day, with 20 minutes being the ideal goal.

- If you're unable to walk due to inclement weather and don't have access to an indoor treadmill, alternatives can be to march in place for 5 minutes a few times a day, walk up and down stairs a few times a day (in addition to what you already may be doing), or set a timer and walk throughout your home nonstop.

Lifestyle/Mindset Pillar:
Know your "why."

- Take time to consider this if you don't have a solid "why" for the health goals you would like to achieve.

- Write down your why(s).

- Knowing your deeper why will help keep you going when times get tough in your wellness journey.

Gratitude for the win!

- Write down three things each day for which you're grateful and take a few moments to think about them. Note that it doesn't have to be three different items each day unless you would like to do that.

- Keep the list somewhere visible throughout your day.

Data:
On Day 1 of Week 1

- Take your starting weight and record it.

- Take your waist measurement at your navel and record it. Your waist may be smaller above your navel, but taking the measurement at the navel ensures accurate comparison for future waist measurements (this will be done weekly).

- Take "before" photos of yourself (front, side, and back). Ideally be minimally clothed and keep the photo in a safe place for future reference.

Week 2 (Days 8–14)
Continue Week 1 action items and the following.

Nutrition Pillar:
Eliminate grains!

- Add more vegetables, healthy fats, and fruits to your diet to help you adjust to eliminating grains. (A daily total vegetable-to-fruit ratio of 3 vegetable servings to every 1 fruit serving is recommended.)

- This needs to be a 100% elimination to be an effective reset.

- See "Chapter 14: Helpful Food-Prep Tips for the 28-Day Kickstart Plan" and "Appendix A" for meal ideas.

Consume 90–100 grams of protein daily!

- You can track this manually or get a tracking app (there are free versions available, such as MyFitnessPal).

- If needed, add in a protein smoothie daily to help meet this goal. Follow the recommendations in "Chapter 11: Protein for the Win."

Movement Pillar:
Yoga

- Start a daily yoga practice for 10 minutes a day.

- The best time of day to do yoga? Whenever you're most likely to get it done. Some like to do it first thing in the morning, others at night—whenever you will do it regularly is the best time.

- Look up yoga videos on YouTube and include special parameters in your search such as "10-minute yoga" and "beginner yoga."

- As always, honor your body's abilities and limitations. Don't do a posture/stretch if it's uncomfortable. Be gentle with yourself.

Lifestyle/Mindset Pillar:
Breathing practice for stress management

- Implement a breathing practice at least once a day. For breathing practice information, see "Chapter 5: Where Do You Land on the 'Stress-o-Meter'"?

- Do the practice around the same time each day to accustom your brain to it; you can use it as needed throughout the day, but do the daily one as a standard. Attach it to an existing habit, such as brushing your teeth, to help you adhere to it. In addition, you can post a note on your mirror as a reminder.

Data:
On Day 1 of Week 2 (Day 8)

- Take your weight and record it.
- Take your waist measurement at your navel and record it.

Week 3 (Days 15–21)

Continue Weeks 1 and 2 action items and add the following.

Nutrition Pillar:
Eliminate Dairy!

- Prep for this. Have nut milks and/or coconut milk alternatives ready as needed.
- Have non-dairy calcium foods ready.
- And remember, you'll survive without dairy for 30 days.

Eliminate Industrial Vegetable and Seed Oils!

- Remove these items from your pantry and replace them with the healthy, "safe" oil options discussed in "Chapter 8: Ditch the Diet Fads."

Movement Pillar:

- Do squats and planks 3 times a week. You can do these on Mondays, Wednesdays, and Fridays, or Tuesdays, Thursdays, and Saturdays. Just be sure to complete them 3 times a week and have at least one rest day in between each exercise day.
- Do modified versions of squats and planks as needed. See the exercise instructions provided in "Chapter 13: Let's Get Physical" for examples.

- Complete 45 squats at each session.
  - Break up the squats into 3 sets of 15 with 60 seconds of rest between sets. If that's too intense for your current fitness level, decrease the sets and reduce the reps as needed (and increase rest times as needed).
  - If needed, you can start with 5–10 squats total done 3 times a week, depending on your fitness level, and incrementally work your way up.
- Complete 3 planks at each session.
- Do 3 sets of planks with a 30 second rest between sets (take a longer rest if needed) daily.
  - You can start with holding the plank for 5–10 seconds and incrementally increase to 30 seconds (or beyond if your fitness level is high).
- It's best to do squats and planks after your body has been warmed up—for example, after your walk.
  - Or do "knee ups," "butt kickers," or march in place for 3 minutes to warm up your body.
  - If you go with one of these options, you can do 3 sets of 1 minute each with a 30 second rest in between, and if that's too much, you can break it down to 6 sets of 30 seconds each with a 30 second rest. Take longer rest periods if needed.
- After completing the squats and planks exercises, it would be ideal to do your 10 minutes of yoga or the stretches provided in "Chapter 13: Let's Get Physical."

Lifestyle/Mindset Pillar:

- If you're not sleeping optimally—not long enough or you have poor quality, such as waking up often, being a light sleeper, or waking up early and being unable to go back to sleep—try one (or more) of the sleeping tips given in "Chapter 6: Are You Counting Sheep?"

- Keep in mind that what works for one person may not work well for another. However, do give each tip a chance before going on to another (give it a week, as your body needs to adjust; for example, your brain may initially resist the "screen curfew" because it wants the "dopamine hits" provided by what is viewed on the screens).

Data:
On Day 1 of Week 3 (Day 15)

- Take your weight and record it.
- Take your waist measurement at your navel and record it.

Week 4 (Days 21–28)

Continue Weeks 1, 2, and 3 action items and add the following.

Nutrition Pillar:
Intermittent fasting!

- Remove an hour from your normal eating window. Incrementally increase your fasting window by one hour each week, and make the 16:8 fasting/eating window your goal.

- Note that even a 12:12 fasting/eating window has benefits. If you don't make it to 16:8, you are still getting some benefits.

Movement Pillar:
More home exercises!

- These exercises are done in addition to the squats and planks you started last week.

- It's best to do exercises after your body has been warmed up—for example, after your walk.
  - Or do "knee ups," "butt kickers," or march in place for 3 minutes to warm up your body.
  - If you go with one of these options, you can do 3 sets of 1 minute each with a 30 second rest in between, and if that's too much, you can break it down to 6 sets of 30 seconds each with a 30 second rest. Take longer rest periods if needed.

- Do the exercises provided in "Chapter 13: Let's Get Physical" as indicated below 3 days a week. These can be done on the same days you do your squats and planks. As with the squats and planks, have at least one rest day in between each exercise day.

- Here are the exercises to be added this week. Refer to "Chapter 13" for specifics for each exercise. Also, note that a wide range of reps is provided so you can adjust to your individual fitness level accordingly.
  - Double leg-drop: 3 sets, 5–10 reps each set, 45 second rest in between sets.
  - Bicycle crunch: 3 sets, 8–15 each side for each set, 45 second rest in between sets.
  - Glute bridge: 3 sets, 8–12 reps each set, 45 second rest in between sets.

- ○ Kneeling push-ups: 3 sets, 3–8 each set, 45 second rest in between sets, or do wall push-ups if the knee push-ups are too intense (same sets, reps, and rest as the kneeling option).

- ○ Standing arm front raises: 3 sets, 6–12 reps each set, 45 second rest in between sets.

- ○ Standing arm lateral raises: 3 sets, 6–12 reps each set, 45 second rest in between sets.

- ○ Forward lunge: 3 sets, 6–12 each side for each set, 45 second rest in between sets.

- ○ Reverse lunge: 3 sets, 6–12 each side for each set, 45 second rest in between sets.

- If any exercise is too intense for your current fitness level, you can:
  - ○ Reduce the reps and/or
  - ○ Increase your rest time in between sets and/or
  - ○ if still too difficult, start with doing 1 set total and decrease the reps by half (or less if needed).

- After completing your exercise routine, you can either do 10 minutes of yoga as a post-exercise stretch routine or do some basic post-exercise stretches, as follows. (Refer to "Chapter 13" for the specifics for each stretch.)
  - ○ Knee to chest: Hold 15–30 seconds each side; 1 set.
  - ○ Quad stretch (either standing or lying down): Hold 15–30 seconds each side; 1 set.
  - ○ Supine figure-four hip stretch: Hold 15–30 seconds each side; 1 set.
  - ○ Shoulder rolls: Roll backward for 5 rolls, then roll forward for 5 rolls and repeat both directions for a second set.

○ Shoulder cross stretch: Hold for 15–30 seconds each side; 1 set.

Lifestyle/Mindset Pillar:
Meditation!

- Try out meditation daily.
- Start with 5 minutes a day with a goal of increasing it to 10 minutes.
  - ○ 20 minutes is the ultimate goal, but if you don't get past 5–10 minutes, you're still getting benefits, and I encourage you to keep doing it daily at the 5–10-minute mark.
  - ○ Doing meditation anytime of the day that you will get it done is the best time.
- Check out these apps: Insight Timer (free with option to purchase) and Calm (offers a free 7-day trial).

Data:
On Day 1 of Week 4 (Day 22)

- Take your weight and record it.
- Take your waist measurement at your navel and record it.

On Day 7 of Week 4 (Day 28)

- Take your weight and record it.
- Take your waist measurement at your navel and record it.
- You can take progress pictures at this point (front, side, and back).

Your journey isn't over, however: the 28-day plan is a kickstart into your path to optimal wellness!

CONCLUSION

*C*ongratulations on completing this book and taking the first step toward improving your health. You've gained valuable knowledge and tools you can use to make a positive change in your life. As you move forward, here are some important tips to keep in mind:

1. **Focus on What's Included.** Embrace the wonderful elements of this plan and concentrate on what you can do, rather than what you can't. Shift your mindset to one of empowerment, knowing that you have the ability to make healthy choices that will serve you well.

2. **Adopt an "I Get To" Mindset.** Change the way you think about your journey. Instead of feeling obligated by an "I have to..." mentality, adopt an "I get to..." attitude. See each choice as an opportunity to enhance your well-being and create positive effects in your life.

3. **Celebrate Every Win.** Acknowledge and celebrate all your wins, big or small. Every step forward is progress, and each small victory contributes to the bigger picture of your health journey. Remember, even the tiniest successes can open the door to significant transformations.

4. **Embrace the Journey.** Life is a gift, and you have the chance to live it to the fullest. Take care of your body and

its health, as it is the vessel that carries you through this one precious life. Don't wait until things reach a breaking point; start making positive changes now.

5. **Believe in Yourself.** You are capable of achieving incredible things. Trust in your abilities, and always believe in yourself. With dedication and a positive mindset, you have the strength to overcome any obstacles that come your way.

Remember, this is your journey, and you have the power to shape it into a beautiful and fulfilling experience. I believe in you, but most importantly, believe in yourself. You have all the tools and knowledge you need to succeed. Keep going, stay determined, and know that you've got this. Here's to a healthier and happier you!

APPENDIX A

RECIPES

Breakfast Time!

When you remove grains and dairy from your diet, it can seem challenging at first to come up with breakfast ideas, but you'll see that there are a number of delicious options!

Spinach & Sausage Egg Muffins

Ingredients

2¼ tsp avocado oil (or use avocado oil spray)

4⅓ oz pork sausage (casing removed)

3 cups baby spinach (chopped)

4 eggs

2 tbsp water

⅛ tsp sea salt

½ stalk green onion (chopped)

Directions

1. Preheat the oven to 350°F (176°C) and grease a muffin tray with the oil or use a silicone muffin tray.

2. In a pan over medium-high heat, cook the sausage until no longer pink, about 5 to 8 minutes. Break it up into little pieces as it cooks. Drain the excess drippings from the pan and stir in the spinach. Cook until the spinach has wilted and then remove the pan from heat to let cool slightly.

3. In a mixing bowl, whisk the eggs together with the water and sea salt. Fold in the green onion.

4. Divide the sausage mixture evenly into the prepared muffin tray and pour in the egg mixture. Bake for 15 to 18 minutes until the egg is firm to the touch and just brown around the edges. Let the egg muffins cool slightly before removing them from the tray. Enjoy!

Notes

Leftovers: Refrigerate in an airtight container for up to 3 days.

Serving Size: A serving is 2 egg muffins.

More Flavor: Add chili flakes, black pepper, or hot sauce to the eggs. Use milk of choice instead of water (if dairy sensitive or undergoing a dairy-free reset, use non-dairy milk such as almond milk or coconut milk).

Make it Vegetarian: Omit the sausage.

No Sausage: Use ground pork, turkey, or chicken instead. Season the ground meat with additional salt.

No Spinach: Use kale or chard instead.

Vanilla Protein Pancakes

Ingredients

2 bananas (plus extra for topping)

4 eggs

½ cup vanilla protein powder

1 tbsp coconut oil

Directions

1. In a large bowl, mash the bananas. Add the eggs and protein powder. Mix well until a batter forms.

2. Melt the coconut oil in a large skillet over medium heat. Once hot, pour the batter into the skillet, roughly ¼ cup at a time. Cook for 3 minutes, or until the top starts to bubble slightly, and flip. Repeat the process until all the batter is used up.

3. Transfer to a plate and top with additional banana slices. Enjoy!

Notes

Leftovers: Refrigerate in an airtight container for up to 3 days. Freeze for up to 1 month.

Serving Size: A serving is approximately 2 pancakes.

Additional Toppings: Honey, maple syrup, nut butter, chopped nuts, and/or sugar-free chocolate chips (preferably sweetened with stevia).

Easy Turkey Breakfast Sausage

Ingredients

1 lb ground turkey

2 tsp ground sage

2 tsp dried thyme

¼ tsp garlic powder

½ tsp sea salt

1 tbsp coconut oil (or avocado oil)

Directions

1. In a large mixing bowl, combine all ingredients. Form the mixture into even patties.

2. Melt the coconut (or avocado) oil in a large skillet over medium-high heat. Cook the patties about 4 minutes per side depending on thickness, or until cooked through (internal temperature of 165°F (74°C)). Let cool before serving. Enjoy!

Notes

Serving Size: This recipe specifies 6 servings, but make the patties' size (and the total servings) to your preference. I often double or triple this recipe for batch cooking and divide the patties to approximately 3½ oz each in size.

No Turkey: Use ground pork, chicken, bison, or beef instead.

Leftovers: Store in an air-tight container for up to 3 days in the fridge, or separated by parchment or wax paper in a freezer-safe bag in the freezer for up to 3 months.

Additional Flavor: Add in ¼–½ cup of finely chopped green apple into the meat mixture for additional flavor.

Kale & Red Pepper Frittata

Ingredients

8 eggs

½ cup unsweetened almond milk (see "notes" below for substitutions)

½ tsp sea salt

½ tsp black pepper

1 tbsp avocado oil

2 cups kale leaves (chopped)

1 red bell pepper (chopped)

1 cup cherry tomatoes (halved)

Directions

1. Preheat oven to 400°F (204°C).

2. Whisk the eggs, almond milk, salt, and pepper together in a mixing bowl. Set aside.

3. Heat the oil in a cast-iron skillet over medium heat. Add the kale, pepper, and tomatoes. Cook for 5 to 7 minutes, or until the kale is wilted and peppers are tender.

4. Pour the whisked eggs into the pan with the vegetables and let the eggs begin to set for about 30 seconds, before gently stirring with a spatula to ensure the vegetables are well incorporated into the eggs. Transfer the skillet to the oven and bake for 12 to 15 minutes, or until the eggs have set.

5. Remove the skillet from the oven and let sit for about 5 minutes before cutting into wedges. Serve and enjoy!

Notes

No Kale: Use spinach instead.

No Red Bell Pepper: Use a bell pepper of another color instead.

Leftovers: Keep in the fridge for up to 3 days.

Almond Milk Substitutions: Use unsweetened coconut milk, or use heavy cream if not dairy sensitive or undergoing a dairy-free reset.

Grain-Free Coconut Almond Porridge

Ingredients

1½ cups unsweetened almond milk

½ cup almond flour

½ cup unsweetened shredded coconut

2 tbsp ground flaxseed

1 tsp cinnamon (see "notes" below for alternatives to cinnamon)

Directions

1. Add all of the ingredients to a saucepan over medium heat. Whisk continuously until your desired thickness is reached, about 3 to 5 minutes.

2. Divide into bowls and enjoy!

Notes

No Almond Milk: Use unsweetened coconut milk, cashew milk, or hemp milk.

Serving Suggestion: Serve with a side of blueberries, strawberries, raspberries, or blackberries.

Like It Sweet? Add maple syrup or honey.

Cinnamon Replacements: Use allspice, nutmeg, or ginger.

Leftovers: Refrigerate in an airtight container for up to 3 to 5 days.

Serving Size: A serving is equal to approximately 1¼ cups of porridge.

Butternut Squash & Apple Hash with Eggs

Ingredients

2 tbsp avocado oil (divided)

1⅓ cups butternut squash (peeled and chopped into 1-cm cubes)

⅓ cup red onion (chopped)

⅛ tsp sea salt

1 apple (small, finely chopped)

1⅓ cups kale leaves (chopped)

⅛ tsp cinnamon

4 eggs

Directions

1. Heat ⅔ of the oil in a skillet over medium heat. Add the butternut squash and onion and cook, stirring often, for 10 to 12 minutes until the squash is tender. Season with the salt.

2. Add the apple and kale leaves and continue to cook until the kale has wilted down and the apple is warmed through and just tender, about 3 to 5 minutes. Add the cinnamon and stir to combine. Season with additional salt if needed.

3. In a second pan, heat the remaining oil over medium heat. Crack the eggs into the pan and cook until the whites are set and the yolks are cooked to your liking.

4. Divide the breakfast hash between plates and top with an egg. Enjoy!

Notes

Leftovers: Refrigerate the breakfast hash in an airtight container for up to 5 days. The eggs are best enjoyed freshly cooked.

Serving Size: One serving is approximately 1 cup of breakfast hash and 2 eggs.

More Protein: Add in cooked sausage, chicken, or bacon.

Apple: This recipe was created and tested using Spartan apples.

Consistency: Chop the butternut squash and apples into similar size cubes to ensure even cooking.

No Red Onion: Use a yellow or sweet onion instead.

Spinach Quiche with Sweet Potato Crust

Ingredients

1 sweet potato (sliced into thin rounds)

¾ tsp coconut oil (or avocado oil)

7 eggs

3 garlic cloves (minced)

8 stalks green onion (chopped)

4 cups baby spinach (chopped)

1 tomato (diced)

sea salt and black pepper (to taste)

Directions

1. Preheat oven to 425°F (218°C). Grease a glass pie plate with a bit of coconut oil. Cover the base and sides of the plate with the sweet potato rounds. Layer the rounds until no glass is showing. Bake in the oven for 15 minutes.

2. Meanwhile, crack eggs into a mixing bowl and whisk well. Set aside.

3. Heat coconut oil in a skillet over medium heat. Add minced garlic and green onions. Sautée for 3 to 5 minutes. Add chopped spinach and sauté just until wilted. Remove from heat.

4. Add spinach mix and diced tomatoes to the egg mix. Season with salt and pepper. Stir well.

5. Remove sweet potato crust from the oven. Pour egg mixture over top of the crust. Reduce the temperature of the oven to 375°F (191°C). Place quiche in the oven and bake for 30 to 40 minutes or until the top is golden brown.

6. Remove from oven and cut into slices. Enjoy!

Notes

Pie Plate: This recipe was developed and tested using a 9-inch glass pie plate.

Smoothies!

Protein smoothies are a great breakfast or snack option. As mentioned in "Chapter 11: Protein for the Win!", don't make your smoothies "fruit heavy." Here are some recipes to get you started.

Spinach Protein Smoothie

Ingredients

1½ cups baby spinach

½ avocado

½ cup strawberries (frozen or fresh; approx. 70–75 grams or ½ cup)

1 oz vanilla protein powder (use 1 serving per what is stated on the label, may substitute collagen peptide powder)

6 fl oz water (add more or use less water as desired)

5 ice cubes (add more or use less as desired)

Directions

1. Combine all ingredients in a blender and blend until smooth. Enjoy!

Notes

Substitute for Protein Powder: Replace with collagen peptide powder if desired.

A Note About Whey Protein Powder: Whey protein can cause inflammation for some people. If you are on a health or weight loss program, I recommend avoiding whey protein powders until you've met your goals. Reintroduce at that time and monitor for response (weight gain, new pain anywhere on the body, headache, increased intensity of existing pain, digestive issues, etc.).

Need More Greens in Your Day? Double the spinach for extra greens in your day (this is what I do!) and/or add in a greens powder for an additional boost.

Green Pineapple Ginger Smoothie with Aloe

Ingredients

1 cup water

1½ fl oz pure aloe juice

½ cup kale leaves (finely chopped)

2 tsp ginger (peeled and grated)

1 cup frozen pineapple (chunks)

½ avocado (fresh or frozen)

4 ice cubes

⅔ oz vanilla protein powder

Directions

1. Add water, aloe, kale, and ginger to a high-speed blender and blend until kale is pureed.

2. Add remaining ingredients and blend until smooth. Serve immediately.

Notes

No Aloe Juice: Use fresh aloe leaf gel or coconut water instead.

Like It Sweet? Add raw honey to taste.

Collagen Green Smoothie

Ingredients

1 cup water

2 cups baby spinach

½ avocado

½ banana (frozen)

½ oz collagen powder

Directions

1. Place all ingredients in your blender and blend until smooth. Pour into a glass and enjoy!

Notes

No Collagen Powder: Omit or use protein powder instead.

No Spinach: Use kale or romaine lettuce instead.

Make It Vegan/Vegetarian: Omit the collagen and use a plant-based protein powder instead.

Leftovers: Best enjoyed immediately.

Post-Workout Green Smoothie

Ingredients

2 tbsp protein powder (vanilla, or use 20 grams of collagen powder)

1 cup water (cold)

½ avocado

½ banana (frozen)

1 cup baby spinach

Directions

1. Combine all ingredients in a blender and blend until smooth. Divide into glasses and enjoy!

Notes

No Spinach: Use kale instead.

No Protein Powder: Use 20 grams collagen powder or add a few spoonfuls of hemp seeds.

Mint Ginger Green Smoothie

Ingredients

1 cup water (cold)

2 tbsp lemon juice

1 cup baby spinach

½ avocado (frozen)

¼ cup mint leaves (fresh, roughly chopped)

1 tsp ginger (fresh, roughly chopped)

⅔ oz collagen powder

Directions

1. Place all ingredients in your blender and blend until smooth. Pour into a glass and enjoy!

Notes

Like It Sweet? Add frozen banana, pineapple, or apple.

Leftovers: Refrigerate in an airtight container for up to 1 day.

Chocolate Avocado Smoothie

Ingredients

¼ avocado

1 cup unsweetened almond milk

1 tbsp almond butter

1 cup baby spinach

¼ cup chocolate protein powder

Directions

1. Place all ingredients in your blender and blend until smooth. Pour into a glass and enjoy!

Notes

No Chocolate Protein Powder: Use vanilla protein powder or hemp seeds and add cocoa powder.

Like It Sweet? Add frozen banana.

Nut-Free Version: Use coconut milk instead of almond milk and sunflower seed butter instead of almond butter.

Strawberry Coconut Collagen Smoothie

Ingredients

1 cup organic coconut milk (full-fat, from the can)

½ cup water

1 banana (frozen)

1 cup frozen strawberries

⅔ oz collagen powder

2 tbsp unsweetened shredded coconut

½ tsp vanilla extract

Directions

1. Place all ingredients in your blender and blend until smooth. Pour into a glass and enjoy!

Notes

Leftovers: Refrigerate in an airtight container for up to 1 day or freeze into popsicles to enjoy later.

More Flavor: Add honey or maple syrup to taste. Garnish with more shredded coconut.

Make It Vegan: Omit the collagen powder.

More Veggies: Add spinach, kale, frozen cauliflower, or zucchini.

No Collagen: Use protein powder instead.

Blueberry Protein Smoothie

Ingredients

½ cup vanilla protein powder

2 cups frozen blueberries

4 cups baby spinach

1 avocado

1½ cups water (cold)

Directions

1. Place all ingredients in your blender and blend until smooth. Pour into a glass and enjoy!

Notes

No Blueberries: Use any type of frozen berry instead.

Blueberry Energy Smoothie

Ingredients

½ cup cashews

2 cups water

2 cups baby spinach

1⅓ oz collagen powder (or use 2 serving sizes of brand specifications)

1½ cups frozen blueberries

Directions

1. Combine cashews and water in a blender. Blend until very smooth.
2. Add in baby spinach, collagen powder, and frozen blueberries. Blend again until smooth. Divide into glasses and enjoy!

Notes

Collagen Powder Flavor: Use either unflavored or vanilla collagen powder.

Chocolate Cauliflower Shake

Ingredients

2 cups frozen cauliflower

1 banana (frozen)

2 tbsp almond butter

¼ cup cacao powder

½ cup chocolate protein powder

2 cups unsweetened almond milk

½ tsp cinnamon

Directions

1. In your blender, combine all ingredients. Blend until smooth, pour into glasses and enjoy!

Notes

Make It Mocha: Replace half of the almond milk with chilled coffee.

Like It Sweeter? Add pitted Medjool dates.

Lunch and Dinner Recipes

Taco Salad with Beef

Ingredients

10 oz ground beef

1 tbsp chili powder

1½ tsp cumin

½ tsp sea salt

½ cup cherry tomatoes (chopped)

½ jalapeño pepper (chopped)

1 stalk green onion (optional, chopped)

2 tbsp lime juice (divided)

1 head romaine hearts (chopped)

2 tbsp extra virgin olive oil

1 avocado (sliced)

Directions

1. In a pan over medium-high heat, brown the beef. Break the meat into very small pieces with a spatula and cook until no longer pink, about 5 minutes. Drain any excess drippings, but keep the beef in the pan.

2. Add the chili powder, cumin, salt, tomatoes, jalapeño, and green onion (if using) to the beef. Stir to combine. Cook for another 5 minutes until tomatoes are very soft. Remove from heat and stir in half of the lime juice. Season with additional salt if needed.

3. In a large mixing bowl, toss the chopped romaine lettuce with olive oil and remaining lime juice.

4. To assemble the salad, divide lettuce between plates and top evenly with beef and avocado. Serve immediately and enjoy.

Notes

Other Protein Options: Use ground turkey or ground chicken instead of beef if desired.

Other Serving Option: Serve on a bed of cauliflower rice instead of the romaine.

More Flavor: Top salad with additional tomatoes, sliced jalapeños, green onions, salsa, cilantro, lime juice, or hot sauce.

Storage: Refrigerate beef and lettuce separately in airtight containers for up to 3 days.

Greek Chicken Salad

Ingredients

2 tbsp Greek seasoning (or Italian seasoning)

1 lemon (juiced)

¼ cup avocado oil

1¼ lb chicken breast (boneless, skinless)

3 cups cherry tomatoes (halved)

1 cucumber (diced)

¼ cup red onion (finely diced)

1 cup pitted kalamata olives (chopped)

3 tbsp balsamic vinegar

¼ cup extra virgin olive oil

sea salt and black pepper (to taste)

Directions

1. Combine the Greek seasoning, lemon juice, and avocado oil in a shallow bowl or Ziploc bag. Add the chicken breasts and marinate for 20 minutes or overnight.

2. Preheat a grill or skillet over medium heat. Remove chicken from the marinade and cook for 10 to 15 minutes per side, or until chicken is cooked through.

3. While the chicken is cooking, make the salad by combining the cherry tomatoes, cucumbers, red onion, olives, balsamic vinegar, olive oil, salt, and pepper. Mix well.

4. Divide the salad and chicken between plates. Enjoy!

Notes

Cheese Lover: Sprinkle with feta cheese if not dairy-sensitive or undergoing a dairy-free reset.

Salmon Salad Lettuce Wraps

Ingredients

15 oz canned wild salmon (drained)

1 cup unsweetened coconut yogurt

¼ cup fresh dill (minced)

1 tbsp lemon juice

¼ tsp sea salt

½ head green lettuce (separated into leaves and washed)

Directions

1. In a bowl, combine the salmon, coconut yogurt, dill, lemon juice, and salt. Adjust flavors as desired.

2. Scoop the mixture onto the lettuce leaves and enjoy!

Notes

Leftovers: Refrigerate the salmon mixture and lettuce leaves in separate airtight containers for up to 3 days.

Serving Size: A serving equals approximately 3 salmon-stuffed lettuce leaves.

Additional Toppings: Add cucumber, celery, red onion, or tomato.

No Coconut Yogurt: Use a good quality mayonnaise (without soybean or canola oil, such as Sir Kensington or Primal Kitchen brands) and adjust lemon juice and salt as needed. Or, if not dairy sensitive and not undergoing a dairy-free reset, use unsweetened plain Greek yogurt.

Cleaned-Up Chicken Salad

Ingredients
12 oz chicken breast, cooked

12 stalks celery (diced)

½ cup grapes (halved)

4 cups kale leaves (finely sliced into ribbons)

¼ cup slivered almonds

1 tbsp hemp seeds

2 tbsp Dijon mustard

2 tbsp extra virgin olive oil

½ lemon (juiced)

sea salt and black pepper (to taste)

Directions

1. Shred your oven-baked chicken breasts using a cheese grater and place in bowl. Then add celery, grapes, hemp, slivered almonds, and kale to bowl.

2. In a separate small bowl, combine mustard, lemon juice, and olive oil. Stir well.

3. Add dressing to the bowl with chicken and toss well to coat. Season with salt and pepper. Enjoy!

Notes

No Kale: Use other leafy greens as desired.

Deconstructed Burger Bowl

Ingredients

1 lb ground beef

1 tbsp Italian seasoning

1 tsp chili powder (more or less as desired)

1 tsp cumin

1 tsp sea salt

½ tsp black pepper

½ cup mayonnaise (see "notes" below for mayonnaise recommendations)

1 tbsp Dijon mustard (more or less as desired)

1 head romaine hearts (chopped)

1 cup cherry tomatoes (chopped)

6 stalks green onion (optional; chopped, green tops only)

Directions

1. In a pan over medium-high heat, brown the beef. Break the meat into small chunks with a spatula and cook until no longer pink, about 5 minutes. Drain any excess drippings, but keep the beef in the pan.

2. Add the Italian seasoning, chili powder, cumin, salt, and pepper to the beef and stir to combine. Season with additional salt and pepper if needed.

3. In a small bowl, combine the mayonnaise and Dijon mustard.

4. Divide the lettuce, tomatoes, and onion (if using) between bowls and top with cooked beef and the Dijon mayo. Enjoy!

Notes

Mayonnaise: Avoid using mayonnaise with soybean and/or canola oils. Use a quality brand such as Sir Kensington or Primal Kitchen.

More Flavor: Add garlic powder, onion powder, ground coriander, or your favorite steak spice blend to the ground beef.

Additional Toppings: Top bowls with your favorite burger toppings, such as chopped pickles, sauerkraut, ketchup, relish, or avocado. Or, if not dairy sensitive and not undergoing a dairy-free reset, top with shredded cheddar cheese.

Leftovers: Refrigerate in an airtight container for up to 3 days. For best results, keep the dressing and beef separate from the lettuce and toppings until ready to serve.

Turkey Stir Fry

Ingredients

2 tbsp coconut aminos

1½ tsp honey

2 garlic cloves (minced)

1½ tsp ginger (fresh, grated)

1 tbsp avocado oil

½ yellow onion (large, sliced)

12 oz ground turkey

4 cups coleslaw mix

2 stalks green onion (chopped thinly)

¼ cup cilantro (chopped, plus more for garnish)

Directions

1. Make the sauce by mixing the coconut aminos, honey, garlic, and ginger together in a small bowl or jar. Set aside.

2. Heat the oil in a large skillet over medium-high heat. Add the onions and sauté for 2 to 3 minutes until softened. Add the turkey, breaking it up as it cooks. Cook for 5 minutes.

3. Add the coleslaw mix and cook for 2 minutes or until softened. Add the prepared sauce and cook another 2 minutes to 5 minutes, until well combined and the sauce thickens slightly.

4. Remove from the heat and stir in the green onions and the cilantro. Divide evenly between bowls and enjoy!

Notes

Protein Options: Use ground chicken or pork in place of turkey.

Leftovers: Refrigerate in an airtight container for up to 4 days.

Serving Size: A serving is approximately 2 cups.

BLT Spaghetti

Ingredients

12 slices bacon (can be pork bacon or turkey bacon; use sugar-free bacon)

2 zucchini

1 tbsp avocado oil

1 yellow onion (diced)

2 garlic cloves (minced)

2 cups crushed tomatoes (or 28 oz can)

½ tsp oregano

4 cups baby spinach

1 tsp red pepper flakes (to taste)

⅛ tsp black pepper (to taste)

Directions

1. Preheat oven to 400°F (204°C). Line a baking sheet with parchment paper. Spread the bacon in a single layer across the sheet. Bake in the oven for 15 to 18 minutes, flipping once at the halfway point. Remove from oven and wrap in paper towel to soak up the grease. Let cool and then chop into fine pieces. Set aside.

2. Use a spiralizer to spiralize your zucchini into noodles. If you don't have a spiralizer, you can use a box grater (use the side with bigger holes) or a peeling knife to create long strips. (Tip: For best results, glide the zucchini across the entire length of the box grater with long strokes.)

3. Heat the avocado oil in a large skillet over medium heat. Add the onion and sauté until translucent. Add the minced garlic and sauté for another minute. Then add the crushed tomatoes and oregano. Let simmer for about 20 to 30 minutes or until thickened.

4. Add the bacon, baby spinach, and zucchini noodles and stir for 3 minutes or until noodles are tender and spinach is wilted. Remove from heat.

5. Spoon into bowls and top with red pepper flakes and ground pepper. Enjoy!

Notes

Time Saver: Use pre-spiralized zucchini, which is available in many grocery stores.

Dairy Option: If not dairy sensitive and if not undergoing a dairy-free reset, top with shredded or grated Parmesan cheese.

More Bacon: If you'd like to add in more bacon, go for it!

Grilled Bruschetta Chicken

Ingredients

1 lb chicken breast

sea salt and black pepper (to taste)

3 tomatoes (medium, diced)

½ cup red onion (finely diced)

2 garlic cloves (minced)

1 cup basil leaves (chopped)

1 tbsp extra virgin olive oil

1 tbsp balsamic vinegar

Directions

1. Preheat the grill to medium heat. Add the chicken breasts, season with sea salt and black pepper, and cook for about 10 to 15 minutes per side, or until cooked through.

2. In a small bowl, combine the tomatoes, red onion, garlic, basil, olive oil, and balsamic vinegar. Season with sea salt and black pepper to taste.

3. To serve, top the chicken breasts with the bruschetta mix. Enjoy!

Notes

No Grill: Bake the chicken breasts in the oven at 350°F (177°C) for 30 minutes.

Serve It With: Serve with grilled or roasted vegetables, cauliflower rice, or your favorite leafy green.

Dairy Option: If not dairy sensitive or undergoing a dairy-free reset, sprinkle with feta or mozzarella cheese before serving.

Beef, Sweet Potato, & Broccoli Skillet

Ingredients

10 oz ground beef

½ yellow onion (sliced, optional)

1½ tsp ginger (peeled and grated)

1 garlic clove (minced)

1 sweet potato (medium sized, grated)

½ bunch broccoli (chopped, or sub with rapini)

½ tsp sea salt (to taste)

Directions

1. Heat a large skillet over medium-high heat and add the beef, onion, ginger, garlic, and sweet potatoes. Cover and cook for 10 to 15 minutes, stirring occasionally until the beef is cooked through and the sweet potatoes are soft.

2. Add the broccoli and cook for about 5 more minutes or until greens are wilted and stalks are soft.

3. Divide into bowls. Season with sea salt and enjoy.

Notes

Leftovers: Store leftovers in an airtight container in the fridge for up to 3 days.

Time Saver: Use jarred minced ginger.

One Pan Olive Pesto Pork Chops

Ingredients

1 cup black olives (pitted, rinsed, and patted dry)

1 garlic clove

¾ tsp avocado oil (or substitute with coconut oil)

2 tbsp nutritional yeast

8 oz pork chop

1 cup green beans (stems removed, chopped)

1 cup cherry tomatoes

1 leek (chopped into ½-inch medallions, see "notes" for substitutes)

Directions

1. Preheat oven to 400°F (204°C) and line a baking sheet with foil.

2. In a food processor, combine black olives, garlic, avocado oil, and nutritional yeast until a paste forms. Set aside.

3. Add remaining ingredients to a large mixing bowl. Using your hands, generously coat the pork chops and veggies with the desired amount of olive pesto.

4. Transfer the pork chops and veggies onto the baking sheet in an even layer and bake for 25 minutes, or until pork is cooked through. Divide onto plates and enjoy!

Notes

No Leeks: Use green onions, yellow or white onions, or shallots instead.

Leftover Pesto: If you don't use all the pesto, you can add it to pasta, omelets, or sandwiches, or use as a dip for veggie sticks and crackers.

Storage: Refrigerate in an airtight container up to 3 days.

Sausage & Cauliflower Rice Stuffed Peppers

Ingredients

⅓ cup water

4 yellow bell peppers (or any other color)

1 lb pork sausage (casing removed, see "notes" below for substitutions)

½ yellow onion (chopped)

2 garlic cloves (minced)

1½ tsp Italian seasoning

¼ tsp sea salt

1½ cups cauliflower rice (use pre-riced frozen cauliflower rice)

1 cup tomato sauce (see the "More Flavor" section in "notes" for substitutions)

Directions

1. Preheat the oven to 350°F (176°C). Add the water to the bottom of a baking dish.

2. Cut off the tops of the peppers and discard the seeds and ribs.

3. Heat a pan over medium-high heat. Add the sausage to the pan, breaking it up with a wooden spoon as it cooks. Once it is cooked through and no longer pink, about 8 minutes, drain any excess drippings from the pan.

4. Add the onion, garlic, Italian seasoning, and salt to the pan with the sausage. Cook for 3 to 5 minutes until the onions have softened. Remove the pan from the heat and stir in the cauliflower rice and tomato sauce until well combined.

5. Stuff the peppers with the sausage and cauliflower rice filling. Place the peppers so that they are standing upright in the prepared baking dish. Cover with foil or a lid and bake for 45 to 50 minutes or until the peppers are very tender.

6. Divide between plates and enjoy!

Notes

Pork Sausage Substitutions: Use ground turkey, ground beef, or ground chicken instead. If not using sausage, add Italian seasoning to the ground meat.

More Flavor: Add red pepper flakes for more spice. Use your favorite marinara sauce instead of plain tomato sauce. Use hot or mild Italian-spiced sausage instead.

Peppers Not Staying Upright: Thinly slice the bottom of them to create a flat surface.

Additional Toppings: Top with fresh herbs or serve with extra tomato sauce. Or, if not dairy sensitive or undergoing a dairy-free reset, top with shredded cheese of your choice.

Pan Fried Turmeric Ginger Tilapia

Ingredients

2 tbsp avocado oil

1 lime (juiced)

1 tbsp ginger (peeled and grated)

2 garlic cloves (minced)

1 tsp turmeric (ground)

1 tsp cumin (ground)

1 tsp chili powder

¼ tsp sea salt

4 tilapia fillets (about 6 oz each)

1 tbsp coconut oil (or substitute with avocado oil)

Directions

1. In a small mixing bowl, whisk together avocado oil, lime juice, ginger, garlic, turmeric, cumin, chili powder, and sea salt. Transfer the mixture to a Ziploc bag.

2. Place fish fillets in the bag, press out the extra air, and seal the bag. Using your hands, massage the turmeric-ginger sauce onto each fillet. Let fish marinate for at least 15 minutes or for up to 1 hour.

3. Heat the coconut oil (or avocado oil) in a large skillet or frying pan over medium-high heat. Transfer the fillets from the bag to the pan and cook for 3 to 4 minutes per side until golden brown and crisp. (Note: You may need to cook the fillets in batches depending on the size of your pan.)

4. Transfer the fillets to a plate and season with additional salt if needed. Enjoy!

Notes

Extra Flavor: Serve with lemon, lime, or orange wedges.

Like It Spicy? Add cayenne pepper to the marinade to taste.

No Tilapia: Use any type of white fish fillet instead, such as cod, haddock, pickerel, or orange roughy. Cooking times may vary depending on the thickness of the fillet.

Meal Prep: Combine the marinade and fish together in a bag and freeze for up to 3 months. Thaw before cooking.

Time Saver: Use jarred minced ginger.

One Pan Lemon Chicken with Asparagus

Ingredients

1½ tsp avocado oil

10 oz chicken breast (boneless, skinless, cubed)

2 cups asparagus (woody ends trimmed, chopped)

1 lemon (juiced and zested)

¼ cup chicken broth

1 tsp tapioca flour

2 garlic cloves (minced)

2 tbsp parsley (chopped)

¼ tsp sea salt

Directions

1. Heat the oil in a pan over medium heat. Add the chicken and cook for about 10 to 12 minutes, stirring occasionally, or until cooked through and browned.
2. Add the asparagus to the pan and cook for another 4 to 5 minutes.

3. In a small bowl, whisk together the lemon juice, lemon zest, broth, and tapioca flour. Add the mixture to the pan along with the garlic and parsley.

4. Stir and season with salt. Cook for about a minute or until thickened, stirring occasionally. Divide evenly between plates and enjoy!

Notes

Leftovers: Refrigerate in an airtight container for up to 3 days.

Serving Size: A serving is equal to approximately 1½ cups.

More Flavor: Add onion, bell pepper, and/or broccoli. Serve over cauliflower rice.

Pineapple Coconut Shrimp

Ingredients

3 garlic cloves (minced)

2 tbsp avocado oil (or substitute with coconut oil)

2 tbsp red wine vinegar

2 tbsp parsley (chopped)

½ tsp sea salt

2 lb shrimp (raw, peeled, and deveined)

4 cups pineapple (diced into chunks)

2 tbsp unsweetened coconut flakes

12 barbecue skewers

Directions

1. In a large bowl, stir together the garlic, oil, red wine vinegar, parsley, and sea salt. Mix well. Add shrimp and toss well to coat.

2. Preheat grill to medium heat.

3. Slide a shrimp onto a skewer, followed by a pineapple chunk. Repeat until all ingredients are used up.

4. Transfer skewers to the grill and cook for 3 to 4 minutes per side or until shrimp is pink. Remove from grill and sprinkle with coconut flakes. Serve over a bed of greens or with your favorite side dishes. Enjoy!

Notes

No Pineapple: Use sliced lemon instead.

Like It Spicy? Add cayenne pepper to the shrimp spice.

LET'S CONNECT!

To continue your health journey, I invite you to follow me on any of the following platforms:

Website:
https://www.dailywellnessforyou.com/

Facebook:
https://www.facebook.com/people/
Barbara-Diaz-de-Leon/100012906970778

Fabulous and Flourishing Women - Midlife & Beyond

Facebook Community:
https://www.facebook.com/groups/345703096467152/

Instagram:
https://www.instagram.com/coachbarbarajean/

LinkedIn:
https://www.linkedin.com/in/barbaradiazdeleon4/

APPENDIX C

～◦◊◦～

RESOURCES

$\mathcal{A}$t the time of this publication, I am not affiliated with any of the products or companies mentioned. I just like to promote quality products!

Meditation Apps:

- Insight Timer https://insighttimer.com
- Calm https://www.calm.com
- Headspace https://www.headspace.com

Book Recommendations:

- *The Hormone Fix: Burn Fat Naturally, Boost Energy, Sleep Better, and Stop Hot Flashes, the Keto-Green Way*, by Anna Cabeca, DO, OBGYN, FACOG
- *Life in the Fasting Lane: How to Make Intermittent Fasting a Lifestyle—and Reap the Benefits of Weight Loss and Better Health*, by Jason Fung, MD, Eve Mayer, and Megan Ramos
- *The Hormone Cure: Reclaim Balance, Sleep, Sex Drive, and Vitality Naturally with the Gottfried Protocol*, by Sara Gottfried, MD

- *The Thyroid Connection: Why You Feel Tired, Brain-Fogged, and Overweight—and How to Get Your Life Back*, by Amy Myers, MD
- *The Paleo Thyroid Solution: Stop Feeling Fat, Foggy, and Fatigued at the Hands of Uninformed Doctors—Reclaim Your Health!* by Elle Russ

Protein:

If you want to take a deeper dive into protein and its importance, I recommend checking out the website of Gabrielle Lyon, DO: https://drgabriellelyon.com/

Essential Oils:

Eric Zielinski, DC, is a great resource for essential oils. Check out his website for valuable information on all things essential oils: https://naturallivingfamily.com/

CBD Products:

FAB CBD offers quality CBD products: https://fabcbd.com/

Collagen Peptide Powder Recommendations:

- Vital Choice https://www.vitalproteins.com/
- Further Food: https://shop.furtherfood.com/

Beef Protein Powders:

Amy Myers, MD: https://www.amymyersmd.com

(Dr. Myers offers a discount for monthly auto-ship plans.)

Peter Osborne, DC: https://www.glutenfreesociety.org/shop/supplements/ meal-replacement/ultra-pure-protein

(Select the "Ultra Pure Protein" version.)

Justin Marchegiani, DC:
https://justinhealth.com/products/trupaleo-protein

Online Meal Companies for Prepared Healthy Foods:

- Green Chef https://www.greenchef.com/
- Pete's Real Food https://www.petesrealfood.com/
- Paleo on the Go (grass-fed meats and they have "Autoimmune Protocol" options if you are following this nutrition plan) https://paleoonthego.com/

Supplement Brand Recommendations:

- Pure Encapsulations
- Designs for Health
- Thorne
- NOW
- Doctor's Best
- Integrative Therapeutics
- Life Extension
- Biotics Research
- Nordic Naturals (for Vitamin D3 and Fish Oils)
- For electrolytes:
  - https://www.traceminerals.com/product/endure-performance-electrolyte
  - https://cynthiathurlow.com/product/simply-hydration-magnesium-charged-electrolyte-concentrate-for-rapid-hydration/

- https://redmond.life/products/re-lyte-electrolyte-mix
- https://nuunlife.com/products/nuun-daily

Autoimmune Disease Resources:

If you have an autoimmune disease, these are valuable resources:

- Amy Myers, MD
  https://www.amymyersmd.com/free#autoimmunity
- Terry Wahls, MD https://terrywahls.com/
- Eileen Laird https://www.phoenixhelix.com/
- Mickey Trescott & Angie Alt
  https://autoimmunewellness.com/

REFERENCES

Chapter 2:

https://www.heart.org/en/health-topics/metabolic-syndrome/about-metabolic-syndrome

Chapter 3:

https://my.clevelandclinic.org/health/diseases/24613-low-progesterone

https://coyleinstitute.com/low-progesterone-symptoms/

https://www.healthline.com/health/high-estrogen

https://thehollandclinic.com/estrogen-dominance-progesterone-deficiency/

Chapter 4:

https://www.nccih.nih.gov/health/placebo-effect

https://www.cancer.gov/publications/dictionaries/cancer-terms/def/nocebo-effect

https://www.self.com/story/gratitude-practice-tips

Chapter 5:

https://www.webmd.com/balance/stress-management/stress-symptoms-effects_of-stress-on-the-body

https://www.apa.org/topics/stress/health

https://health.usnews.com/wellness/articles/ways-stress-makes-you-gain-weight

https://mindworks.org/blog/health-benefits-of-meditation/

https://www.mayoclinic.org/tests-procedures/meditation/in-depth/meditation/art-20045858

https://www.yogajournal.com/lifestyle/health/womens-health/count-yoga-38-ways-yoga-keeps-fit/

https://www.health.harvard.edu/staying-healthy/yoga-benefits-beyond-the-mat/

https://www.medicalnewstoday.com/articles/248433#3

Chapter 6:

https://www.healthline.com/health/sleep-deprivation/sleep-deprivation-stages

https://www.nhlbi.nih.gov/health/sleep-deprivation

https://www.betterhealth.vic.gov.au/health/conditionsandtreatments/sleep-deprivation#symptoms-of-sleep-deprivation-in-adults

Chapter 8:

https://www.naturallynourishedrd.com/podcast/naturally-nourished-episode-72-3-micronutrients-magnesium-vitamin-c-and-glutamine/

https://www.dsengineers.com/en/solutions-for-industries/vegoil-feed-protein-industries/vegetable-oil-refining/

https://www.amymyersmd.com/article/elimination-diet

Chapter 9:

https://www.rb.gy/iat7h (mayoclinic.org)

https://www.dietdoctor.com/low-carb/keto/supplements

Chapter 10:

https://30amedicalspa.com/calories-in-calories-out/

https://www.scripps.org/news_items/4621-can-insulin-resistance-cause-weight-gain

Chapter 11:

https://drgabriellelyon.com/muscle-centric-medicine/

https://drgabriellelyon.com/do-we-really-need-30-grams-of-protein/

https://www.hopkinsmedicine.org/-/media/bariatrics/nutrition_protein_content_common_foods.pdf

Chapter 12:

https://cynthiathurlow.com/

https://youtu.be/PVJCdREj4Og

https://www.medicinenet.com/what_happens_to_you_when_you_fast_for_16_hours/article.htm

https://daveasprey.com/increase-bdnf-brain-health/

https://www.dietdoctor.com/intermittent-fasting/questions-and-answers

https://www.healthline.com/nutrition/does-fasting-release-toxins-in-the-body#1

https://dofasting.com/blog/what-can-drink-during-intermittent-fasting/

https://www.healthline.com/nutrition/16-8-intermittent-fasting

https://www.healthline.com/nutrition/intermittent-fasting-guide

https://www.healthline.com/nutrition/intermittent-fasting-metabolism#

https://www.webmd.com/fitness-exercise/human-growth-hormone-hgh#

https://www.healthline.com/nutrition/does-lemon-water-break-a-fast#other-factors

Chapter 13:

https://evofitness.at/en/resistance-training/

https://www.prevention.com/fitness/a20485587/benefits-from-walking-every-day/

Feel Great in 28!

https://www.yogajournal.com/lifestyle/health/womens-health/count-yoga-38-ways-yoga-keeps-fit/

https://www.health.harvard.edu/staying-healthy/yoga-benefits-beyond-the-mat

ABOUT THE AUTHOR

Barbara Diaz de Leon is a licensed Registered Nurse and a Certified Health Coach through the Primal Health Coach Institute and the Institute of Transformational Nutrition. She is the visionary behind Daily Wellness for You.

Barbara underwent her own extraordinary transformation in body and mind when she reached her fifties. This life-altering experience fueled her passion for empowering other women to achieve similar changes in their lives. After embarking on her own journey of renewal, she launched her coaching practice, focusing on guiding midlife women toward reclaiming their vitality, shedding unwanted pounds, and embracing life to its fullest.

She provides her clients with easy-to-follow strategies in nutrition, exercise, lifestyle, and mindset—sustainable practices that offer lasting results.

Currently residing in Wisconsin with her husband and four feline companions, Barbara finds joy not only in her coaching career but also in an array of activities. These range from tranquil nature walks to the intense preparation required for bikini competitions!

If you would like to connect with Barbara, visit her website: https://www.dailywellnessforyou.com/

www.ingramcontent.com/pod-product-compliance
Lightning Source LLC
Chambersburg PA
CBHW070927210326
41520CB00021B/6829